ARMOURED FIGHTING VEHICLES of the 20TH CENTURY

ARMOURED FIGHTING VEHICLES
of the 20TH CENTURY

Christopher Chant

Illustrated by John Batchelor

TIGER BOOKS INTERNATIONAL
LONDON

This edition published in 1996 by
Tiger Books International PLC, Twickenham
© Graham Beehag Books, Christchurch, Dorset
All rights reserved
Printed and bound in Singapore
ISBN 1-85501-805-5

Contents

Portentous Beginnings

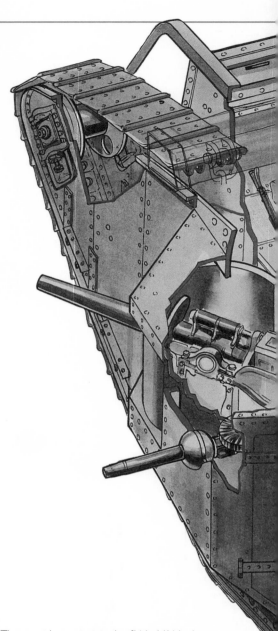

BY November 1914, the mobile phase of World War I (1914-18) had ended, and a system of parallel trench lines, protected by barbed wire entanglements and machine-gun positions, extended between the North Sea and the Swiss frontier to end all chance of mobile warfare until a key could be found to unlock the trench system. In these trench lines German soldiers faced a coalition of Belgian, British and French soldiers, and the tactical method that evolved as each side sought to break the stalemate of this system was the infantry attack supported by artillery bombardment. The preliminary artillery bombardment always failed to cut all the barbed wire and destroy all the machine-gun positions, and thus the infantry assault that followed the artillery bombardment inevitably stalled on the defences or, in the event of an incipient breakthrough, ran out of momentum on ground churned into a quagmire by incessant artillery fire.

What was needed was a new tactical concept, one that would allow a penetration through barbed wire and past machine-gun posts, and would thus obviate the need for a massive and sustained artillery bombardment. The result was the tank, which was the concept of a number of British officers in 1915 and first emerged during December of that year as the Little Willie, which immediately demonstrated its superiority over the original No.1 Lincoln Machine conceptual prototype.

Little Willie was obsolescent even as it appeared, however, for even before the No.1 Lincoln Machine had started its trials, problems were emerging over the basic design's lack of stability when surmounting an obstacle. A new machine was therefore planned as the rhomboidal- or lozenge-shaped tank that became standard in World War I, combining the parapet-climbing superiority of the original but impractical 'bigwheel' concept with the trench-crossing, stability and silhouette advantages of the tracked chassis. The specification for the vehicle, to be called Big Willie, was settled in September.

The building of the new machine was seriously hampered by labour problems at Foster's of Lincoln, where the secrecy of the work was such that the employees could not be given war worker badges, and began to leave when they were accused of cowardice for not having volunteered for the services. During construction the machine was variously called the Wilson Machine, the Centipede, and Big Willie, but finally emerged at the end of 1915 as Mother, which weighed 28.45 tonnes and was powered by a 105hp (78.3kW) Foster-Daimler engine. Built of boiler plate rather than the lightweight pressed steel proposed for the production version, the machine had two lateral sponsons each carrying in its front a naval 6pdr (57mm) quick-firing gun; there were also four machine-guns disposed one in the rear of each sponson, one in the bow and one at the rear. Naval guns were used as the army's Master General of the Ordnance was opposed to the tank concept and therefore refused to release any weapons for use in the new machines.

Mother first ran in December 1915, at about the time that the cover name 'water carrier' (soon amended to 'tank') was ordained at Colonel Ernest Swinton's instigation in preference to the revealing name of 'landship'. After

The most important tank of World War I, the Tank Mk IV was a British type whose development was started in October 1916 for a first run in March 1917, and initial commitment to combat in the Battles of Messines, 3rd Ypres and Cambrai in the second half of 1917. The Mk IV was a development of the original Mk I incorporating a number of lessons learned from the production and combat employment of that type. This cutaway view illustrates the layout of the rhomboidal tank that proved successful in the trench warfare conditions of World War I. The tank had a crew of eight, and its two primary production models were the Tank Mk IV (Male) with a primary armament of two 6pdr (57mm) guns in the forward parts of the sponsons and a secondary armament of four 0.303in (7.7mm) Lewis or 0.315in (8mm) Hotchkiss machine guns, and the Tank Mk IV (Female) with an armament of six machine guns.

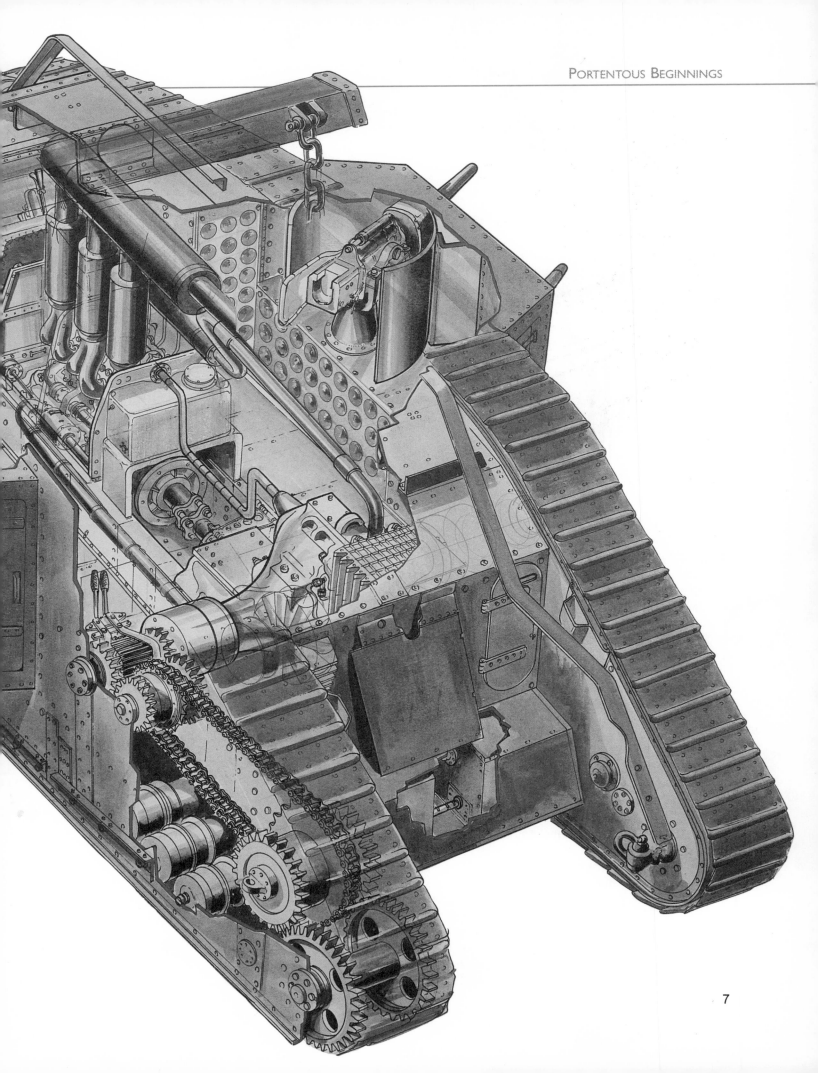

initial and successful running trials, Mother was fully completed in January 1916 and moved, together with Little Willie, to Hatfield Park for two official trials and demonstrations. Both tanks were put through trials in terrain very similar to that of the Western Front (complete with British and German trench layouts), and Mother was judged worthy of production. The Ministry of Munitions had refused to allow tank production in December, but in February the ministry relented, and ordered the production of 100 tanks based on Mother (25 by Foster's and the other 75 by the Metropolitan Carriage, Wagon and Finance Co.).

Winston Churchill, First Lord of the Admiralty and an early advocate of the tank, was now in France, having been forced to resign in May 1915 when a coalition government took over from the Liberal administration after the failure of the Dardanelles campaign. Though now only a regimental officer, Churchill sent to Field Marshal Sir Douglas Haig, the British commander-in-chief in France, a paper entitled 'Variants of the Offensive' which exaggerated the state of tank development and persuaded Haig to despatch Major Hugh Elles to report personally on the new weapon. It was Elles's approval that persuaded Haig to think in terms of an order for 40 tanks that led to the initial plan for 100 vehicles, later increased to 150.

In March 1916 the new tank arm was formed under Swinton, the conceptual father of the tank, initially as the Armoured Car Section, Motor Machine-gun Service, and then from May as the less revealing Heavy Section, Machine-gun Corps. (After the tank had been used in action the name was changed in November 1916 to the Heavy Branch, Machine-gun Corps and in July 1917 to the Tank Corps.) As the men for the new branch were being recruited and trained, production of the service version of Mother, the Tank Mk I, was being undertaken for the first deliveries to be made in June. At first it was planned

The Little Willie was the second tank prototype to be built, and was a development of the No.1 Lincoln Machine with revised trackwork to allow it to cross a 5ft (1.52m) trench and climb a 4ft 6in (1.27m) parapet. The simulated turret of the No.1 Lincoln Machine was removed and the resulting hole in the upper surface plated over, and the machine was generally operated with a pair of rear-mounted steering wheels (not illustrated).

that the production model should be all but identical with Mother, other than construction in mild steel rather than boiler plate and the installation of a frame of wood and chicken wire over the roof to prevent 'bombs' (grenades) from detonating on it.

However, in April 1916 Swinton decided that a proportion of the tanks (ultimately fixed at half of the production run) should be completed with the Hotchkiss 6pdr (57mm) guns replaced by two machine-guns. The more powerful variant was designated Tank Mk I Male, and at a combat weight of 28.45 tonnes carried an armament of two Hotchkiss L/40 guns in limited-movement mountings plus three or four Hotchkiss machine-guns: the role of this variant was to tackle guns, emplacements and other fixed defences. The lighter variant, with a combat weight of 27.43 tonnes, was designated Tank Mk I Female and carried an armament of one or two Hotchkiss air-cooled machine-guns plus four water-cooled Vickers machine-guns (in place of the Male's guns and sponson-mounted machine-guns): the role of this variant was protection of the heavier Males from infantry attack, and pursuit of enemy infantry.

The men of the new army branch were soon coming to grips with their extraordinary new machines, which offered great things but were extremely uncomfortable. The Tank Mk I lacked any form of sprung suspension, vision of the outside world was limited by the small size of the few vision slits, the engine was unsilenced (internal communication had to be undertaken mostly by hand signalling) and ventilation was virtually nonexistent. And, as operations were shortly to confirm, while the tank's construction (soft steel that was cut and drilled and then hardened before being bolted together) may have provided protection from small-arms fire, it was prone to spall and splash when struck on the outside. The crew had to wear thick clothing and face protection to avoid being pierced and cut by shards flying off the inside of the armour when it was struck on the outside (spall), or hit by the molten metal that penetrated the tank's ill-fitting plates when bullets melted upon hitting the tank (splash).

Seen on trials with the rear-mounted pair of steering wheels, the Little Willie was decidedly superior to the No.1 Lincoln Machine from which it was developed, but was already obsolescentin concept by the time it appeared as the immediate future lay with the rhomboidal tank with tracks running round considerably larger track frames on each side of the vehicle.

The tank went into action for the first time in September 1916 in one of the subsidiary components of the Battle of the Somme, namely the Battle of Flers-Courcelette: here the British Reserve and 4th Armies were to punch a 4 mile (6.4km) hole in the German line at Flers and Courcelette in the sector between Thiépval and Combles, the 10 assault divisions being supported by a proposed 50 tanks. Yet such was the technical infancy of the new weapon that some 18 Mk I tanks had broken down before the assault started, and the surviving 32 machines were allocated in penny packets (the largest number being seven tanks) to lead the infantry into battle with the totally dumbfounded German troops. In the event the tanks did well, but their role was hopelessly misjudged and their effect was minimal.

Although the tanks' actual successes had been poor, their use had finally persuaded the sceptical officers in France that the tank was a potentially decisive weapon. Tank orders were stepped up and tank arm personnel was increased to 9,000 by February 1917 and to 20,000 by the time of the Armistice in November 1918. After Flers-Courcelette, Haig requested the production of another 1,000 tanks. Stern moved swiftly to order the required armour and powerplants, although the limited power of the Foster-Daimler petrol engine led this astute pioneer to consider alternatives to this weakest feature of the Tank Mk I. That the army as a whole was still uncommitted to the tank found expression in the Army Council's October cancellation of Haig's order; however, the order was reinstated by Lloyd George, who was a keen advocate of any device that could reduce the horrific toll of head-on infantry battles. Lloyd George was to become prime minister on 6 December 1916, and Stern persuaded him of the need not only for more tanks but for better tanks. An improved machine was now under development as the Tank Mk IV, but to maintain the production of existing designs, Lloyd George sanctioned the assembly of 100 examples of Tanks Mk II and Mk III, essentially the Mk I with detail modifications. The Mk II (50 built) had a revised roof hatch with raised coaming and wider track shoes at every sixth link for greater traction, while the Mk III (50 built) was the Mk II armoured to the standard of the Mk IV. The Mks II and III complemented the Mk I machines in the trench battles of early 1917, but these first three models were rapidly superseded by the Mk IV during the second half of the year. Once discarded as first-line tanks, the Mks I, II and III were used as training tanks or as wireless tanks (one sponson fitted out as a 'wireless office' and the other carrying the

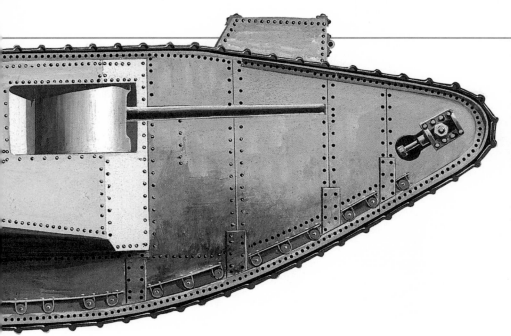

Mother was the true prototype of the basic design concept that became standard for British tanks in World War I. The nature of the tracks running right round rhomboidal frames gave the lower part of the trackwork approximatly the shape and radius of a 60ft (18.3 m) wheel for good trench-crossing and parapet-climbing capability. The revisionof the tracks meant, however, that a superimposed turret would have created centre of gravity problems, and it is this factor that led to the decision to use sponsons located on the outside of the plating that supported the track on each side.

wireless equipment) or, with their sponsons removed and the resultant openings plated over, as supply tanks.

The Tank Mk IV introduced sponsons with upward-swept lower sides, but this more practical design was not carried forward to the supply tenders' panniers. Each supply tank could tow three sleds each carrying 22.40 tonnes of stores, and in the case of Mk IV conversions an uprated 125hp (93.2kW) engine was often fitted to provide greater tractive power. These supply tanks were generally used to ferry forward ammunition and fuel, and to carry back the most seriously wounded.

By February 1917, the Tank Mk IV was ready for production. The type still relied on the indifferent Foster-Daimler engine and its associated gear system, but was otherwise a much improved vehicle incorporating the lessons of Flers-Courcelette. Several of the earlier tanks had suffered because of the gravity feed system from their internal fuel tank, which leaked petrol over the inside of the tank if it was punctured, and failed to work if the tank was ascending or descending a steep parapet. In the Mk IV, the fuel tank was moved to the outside of the vehicle between the rear horns, increased in capacity, provided with armour, and fitted with a pump to ensure an uninterrupted flow of petrol. Other major improvements included the use of thicker armour to defeat the Germans' new anti-tank rifle bullets; steel 'spuds' bolted to every third, fifth or ninth track shoe to increase traction; smaller sponsons that could be shifted inboard rather than removed for transport; an exhaust and external silencer for the engine; improved internal stowage, ventilation and cooling; shorter 6pdr (57mm) L/23 guns to prevent the muzzles digging into the ground; an unditching beam carried above the vehicle on special rails; and 0.303in (7.7mm) Lewis machine-guns in place of the original Hotchkiss weapons in ball-and-socket mountings. Experience soon confirmed that the Lewis gun was unsuitable for tank use as its air-cooling system filled the tank with fumes, the gun itself was vulnerable to enemy fire, and the need for a large opening in the sponson to accommodate the gun's air-cooling jacket increased the problem of splash (a revised Hotchkiss was then substituted, although without the original form of very limited-movement trunnion mounting).

Delivery of Mk IV tanks began in April 1917, and the production of 1,015 tanks was undertaken in the ratio of three female to two male tanks. The Tank Mk IV Female was somewhat different to the earlier females, for the sponsons

were shallower (allowing the incorporation of a pair of hatches on each side in the area previously covered by the sponson) and narrower. The lighter weight of these sponsons contributed significantly to the reduction in combat weight to 26.418 tonnes.

The growing sophistication of the tank is attested by the development of several Mk IV variants as dictated by the nature of combat experience. Possibly the most important of these was the Mk IV Fascine Tank. In its original form this could carry wooden fascines on its unditching beam rails, these chain-bound bundles of brushwood being dropped over the nose under control of the driver; later versions carried hexagonal wood or steel cribs for the same purpose of filling a trench and providing a roadway for the tank's further progress.

The key moment for the Tank Mk IV, and indeed for the tank in general, came in November 1917 with the beginning of the Battle of Cambrai. This was the first occasion in which tanks were used in a homogeneous mass, and the practice nearly proved decisive. The British 3rd Army was entrusted with a surprise offensive against the German 2nd Army: in ideal terrain conditions to the south of Cambrai, the British army was to attack without the protracted artillery bombardment that had previously been standard. This novel concept was designed to give the Germans no forewarning of the offensive, and also to prevent the ground from being churned up, which ensured excellent progress for the 400 tanks that spearheaded the offensive behind a sharp creeping barrage that forced the Germans to keep their heads down. Tactical surprise was achieved by this novel approach, and the tanks were instrumental in opening a 6 mile (9.7km) gap in the German line, through which the British advanced to a depth of 5 miles (8km). Two cavalry divisions were poised to exploit any advantage, but the extent of this success caught the British so unexpectedly that there were insufficient infantry and tanks in reserve to allow any rational exploitation. The Germans recovered with remarkable speed, and their counterattacks from the end of the month forced the British to fall back most of the way to their start line. The Battle of Cambrai was thus a draw,

The order for 100 (later 150) operational tanks based on the design of Mother was placed in February 1916, and resulted in the Tank Mk I that differed from Mother in being fabricated from armour rather than boiler plate, in having a raised frontal cupola for the commander and driver, and in possessing lateral sponsons that could be removed to facilitate rail transport. A problem with this last facility lay in the fact that the tank lacked sufficient torsional rigidity to resist the 'wringing' that could result from this practice, which often made it difficult to re-install the sponsons. The vehicle illustrated here is a Tank Mk I (Male) with a primary armament of two 6pdr (57mm) guns and a secondary armament of four Vickers or Hotchkiss machine-guns. Other details of the eight-man Tank Mk I (Male) included a weight of 28 tons, length of 32ft 6in (9.91m), width of 13ft 9in (4.19m), height of 8ft (2.44m), and speed of 3.7mph (5.95 km/h) on its 105 hp (78.3kW) Daimler-Foster petrol engine.

The tank of World War I was vulnerable to a number of factors including high-velocity bullets fired by special rifles, artillery fire on the rare occasions that such guns could be brought to bear, mechanical breakdown, and the conditions typical of the northern part of the Western Front, where churned ground, mud, shell holes, and the very size of the trench network could bring such vehicles to a halt.

but this cannot disguise the fact that the first mass use of tanks had in general secured unprecedented results.

As usual, however, a large number of tanks had suffered mechanical breakdown, and many tanks were captured by the Germans as they pushed back the British. Impressed with the capabilities of the tanks, and lacking their own counterparts, the Germans rushed the captured machines to their depot at Charleroi for refurbishment and re-arming: the 6pdr (57mm) guns were replaced by Sokol 57mm guns captured from the Russians, and the 0.303in (7.7mm) machine-guns by 7.92mm (0.31in) MG08 weapons. The vehicles were then issued to the Germans' fledgling tank arm with the designation Beutepanzerwagen IV, the comparative extent of British and German tank production at this time being indicated by the fact that captured tanks equipped four of the Germans' seven tank companies in December 1917.

As noted above, Stern appreciated from the early days of the Mk I that the weakest point of the tank was its transmission/gearing and associated Foster-Daimler petrol engine. To meet operational requirements, the Mk IV was rushed into production and service even as Stern was investigating alternative powerplants, and from October 1917 the Tank Supply Department had a modest breathing space in which to consider other tank automotive systems. These included a Wilson mechanical transmission and steering system using epicyclic gears and brakes instead of the standard change-speed gearing, which offered the possibility of one-man control without the potential problems of the petrol-electric systems.

Wilson was entrusted with the overall design of the tank to use his epicyclic gearbox, and this emerged as the Tank Mk V with hull and armament based on those of the Mk IV but fitted with the Wilson gearbox and a new 150hp (112kW) Ricardo petrol engine. The Tank Mk V Male weighed 29.466 tonnes and the Tank Mk V Female 28.45 tonnes, but the use of a more powerful engine and additional fuel tankage boosted maximum speed and range. The Mk V went into production at the Birmingham works of the Metropolitan Carriage, Wagon and Finance Co. during December 1917, and began to reach service

13

Designed as a fast tank to undertake the cavalry role of exploiting any breakthrough created by its larger brethren, the medium tank was based on a higher power/weight ratio, lower trackwork, and a lighter armament operated by a smaller crew. This cutaway view reveals the salient details of the first such type to enter service, namely the Tank Medium Mk A otherwise known as the Whippet or Tritton Chaser, the latter referring to its designer, William (later Sir William) Tritton of William Foster & Co. Ltd. The type first ran in October 1917, and was notable for the location of the engine and fuel tank at the front, with the fighting compartment, carrying three or four Hotchkiss machine-guns with 5,400 rounds of ammunition, at the rear. The other details of the three-man Whippet included a weight of 14 tons, length of 20ft (6.1m), width of 8ft 7in (2.62m), height of 9ft (2.74m), and speed of 8.3mph (13.35 km/h) on its two 45 hp (33.6kW) Tylor JB petrol engines.

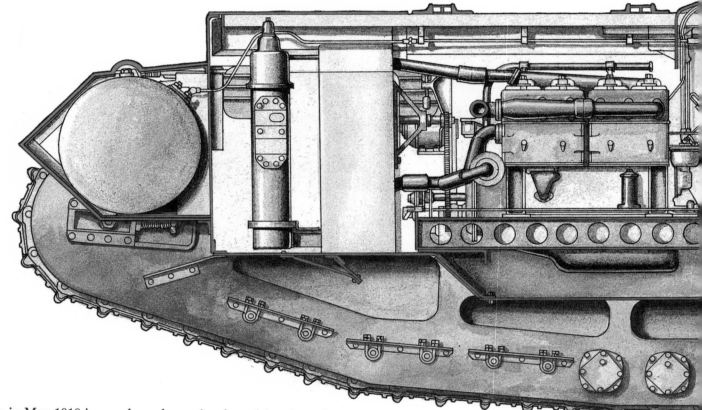

units in May 1918 in equal numbers of male and female tanks, of which a proportion were converted in the field to Tank Mk V Hermaphrodite standard. One-man control of the Mk V's automotive system greatly improved control and manoeuvrability, and the more powerful engine made useful contribution to performance, but the Mk V was also considerably advanced over its predecessors in its better engine cooling and ventilation system; the provision of a cupola above the roof at the rear for the commander, who thus had far better fields of vision than in earlier tanks; and facility for the unditching beam to be connected and disconnected from inside the vehicle, thereby obviating the need for at least two crew members to leave the vehicle.

The Mk V first went into action at Hamel in July 1918, and thereafter partnered the more numerous Mk IV for the rest of World War I. The tank was dimensionally similar to the Mk IV, and suffered the same limitations when faced with a wide trench. Consequently, the Mk V was evaluated with a 'tadpole tail' as pioneered on the Tank Mk IV to improve trench-crossing capability, but a better expedient was adopted after development by the Tank Corps Central Workshops in France from February 1918. This resulted in the Tank Mk V*, in which the vehicle was cut in half to allow the insertion of a

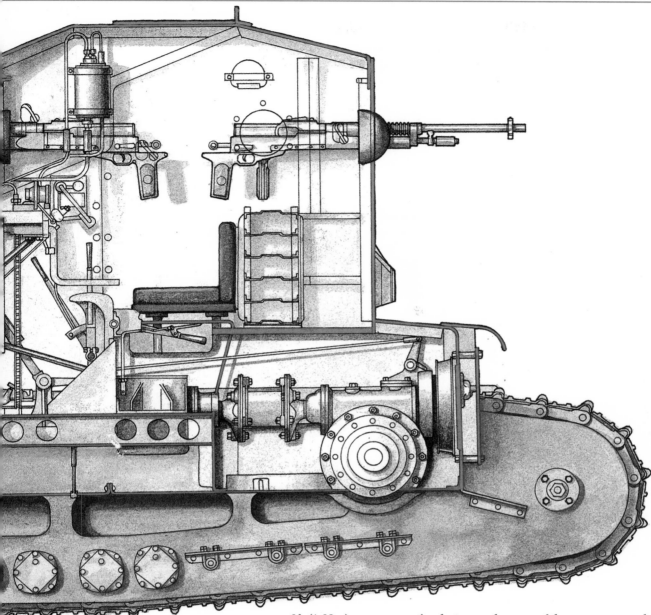

6ft (1.83m) armour section between the rear of the sponsons and the epicyclic gearbox, increasing ground length and providing a 13ft (3.96m) trench-crossing capability, at an increase in weight of 4.064 tonnes. The additional section carried two machine-gun positions to complement the standard fit based on that of the Mk IV, already boosted by the provision of two positions in the new commander's cupola. The extra weight reduced performance slightly and manoeuvrability considerably, but the additional length increased internal volume to the extent that the Mk V* could be used to carry either 25 troops (who suffered badly from the heat and the poor ventilation), or a substantial load of supplies. Production was undertaken by Metropolitan from May 1918, and 579 examples had been built by the time of the Armistice.

The Mk V* was the ultimate version of British mainstream battle tank development to see service in World War I, no fewer than 324 Mk V and Mk V* tanks spearheading the decisive breakthrough offensive of 8 August 1918 in the Battle of Amiens, which the German commander, General Erich Ludendorff, characterized as 'the black day of the German army'. In this offensive the Mk IV and Mk V variants were partnered by a number of light tanks.

The Allied concept of military operations after November 1914 had been posited without significant deviation on a breakthrough of the German line and exploitation into the enemy rear. Even before the battle tank had begun to prove itself as a weapon for the breakthrough phase, tank advocates had begun to work on a lighter and more mobile tank suitable for the exploitation phase, for the battle tank was too slow and too short-ranged for any but the most direct battlefield tasks. In 1916, Tritton designed a high-speed tank with light armour for the task of co-operating with the cavalry, and this initial 'Whippet' scheme was revised from December 1916 as the Tritton Chaser or, more prosaically, the Tritton No.2 Light Machine. The type first ran in February 1917, and trials were generally successful. Various changes were required before a firm order was placed in June 1917. The definitive version became the Medium Tank Mk A, generally named the Whippet, and deliveries from Foster's began in October 1917, to meet the initial requirement for 200 machines. This order was subsequently increased to 385, but then reduced once more to 200 when it became clear that the double automotive system of the Mk A was both expensive to produce and difficult to maintain at a reasonable standard of reliability.

The overall design of the Whippet was totally different to that of the battle tank, with long low-set unsprung tracks whose shoes were based on those of battle tanks but were of lighter construction and fitted with provision for spuds: the tracks were long enough to provide a 7ft (2.13m) trench-crossing capability. The track units were fitted on each side with four chutes along much of the length of the top run to keep the tracks clear of mud. The long forward section of the hull above the upper run of the tracks accommodated two 45hp (33.6kW) Tyler petrol engines, located side by side and each provided with its own clutch and gearbox to drive one track. Twin throttles were located on the steering wheel, their movement together controlling acceleration of this 14.225 tonne vehicle to a maximum speed of 8.3mph (13.4km/h). Movement of the driver's steering wheel worked on the throttles to increase the power of one engine and decrease that of the other (to a maximum variation of 12hp/8.95kW), and so providing additional power to one track or the other. The system was complex and extremely demanding on the driver, who often stalled one engine in a tight turn and then shed a track, thus immobilizing his vehicle.

The fighting compartment at the rear of the vehicle, was essentially a fixed barbette (the original notion of a rotating turret having been abandoned to simplify production), and was occupied by the driver, commander and one or two gunners, and equipped with three or four

The Tank Mk IV (Female) was designed to accompany infantry and to protect the Tank Mk IV (Male) from attack by enemy infantry. It was soon appreciated that such tanks were vulnerable to destruction by the heavier guns carried by German tanks, and a number were therefore adapted to Tank Mk IV (Hermaphrodite) standard with one of the standard machine gun-armed female sponsons replaced by a male sponson carrying one 6pdr (57mm) gun and one machine-gun. Others were adapted to the Tank Mk IV (Fascine) standard illustrated here. This was designed to create passages over the extra-wide trenches of the Germans' Hindenburg Line defences by dropping a fascine: this was a chain-wrapped bundle of wooden rods some 10ft (3.05m) long and 4ft 6in (1.37m)in diameter. Variations on the basic fascine theme were a hexagonal wooden crib and a steel crib.

Medium Tank Mk B Whippet

PRODUCTION of the Medium Tank Mk A was limited to 200 vehicles by the appearance of the more advanced Medium Tank Mk B, which was also nicknamed Whippet. This was based on a new automotive system using a single 100 hp (74.6kW) Ricardo petrol engine located, for the first time in a tank, in a dedicated compartment of its own at the rear of the vehicle and driving the tracks by means of epicyclic gearing. This resulted in greater manoeuvrability, improved reliability and reduced production cost. The Mk B was designed by Major Wilson, and differed from the Mk A in being a larger vehicle based on the rhomboidal shape of the larger tanks with all-round tracks. Mounted on the front of the hull was a large turret :in the Mk B (Male) form that was not built this would have been a revolving unit carrying one 2pdr (40mm) gun, and in the Mk B (Female) form it was a fixed unit carrying four Hotchkiss machine guns with 7,500 rounds of ammunition. Design work was completed late in 1917, but in mid-1918 before an order was placed for 450 such vehicles, of which the first ran in September 1918. Only 45 had been completed by the time of the armistice in November 1918, when further production was cancelled as the Mk B had lower performance than the Mk A, provided cramped conditions for its four-man crew, and offered an engine compartment whose advantages in terms of reduced interior noise and fume levels were offset by a very cramped design that made working on the engine all but impossible unless it was removed.

Hotchkiss machine-guns for all-round fire. The second gunner and the Hotchkiss in the rear of the barbette were usually omitted by operational units to mitigate the appalling conditions inside the barbette.

The type first saw action in March 1918 near Herbertune in northern France, and was used up to the end of the war. The type's greatest moment came in the Battle of Amiens on 8 August 1918, when the 3rd Tank Brigade's two battalions were fully equipped with 96 Mk A machines. The brigade was tasked with support of the Cavalry Corps, and although liaison was poor some useful results were gained. The major tactical problem was apparent in good conditions, when the cavalry was faster than the tank brigade and had to deal with the opposition whilst waiting for the tanks to catch up. As

a result, the tanks were not employed in a homogeneous mass that might have completely destroyed the German rear areas to a depth of 10 miles (16km) or more. The Mk As were used in small numbers attached to specific cavalry units, but nonetheless achieved the successes that fully vindicated their overall capabilities.

The type was limited by its use of two low-powered engines and unsprung tracks, and in an effort to overcome these limitations, Major Philip Johnson, an Army Service Corps officer serving at the Tank Corps Central Workshops in France, reworked the design with sprung tracks and a 360hp (268kW) Rolls-Royce Eagle aero engine working through the transmission of a Mk V battle tank: speeds well over 20mph (32km/h) were achieved, but this important advance failed to find favour.

At much the same time that Colonel Swinton was first pleading his case to the War Office for armoured fighting vehicles, the same pattern of events was emerging in France where Colonel J. E. Estienne had seen the cross-country capability of the Holt tractor and, working from this conceptual basis, advocated the development of what he called a cuirassé terrestre (land battleship) to unlock the static nature of trench warfare. Estienne's ideas found ready acceptance in the mind of General Joseph Joffre, the French field commander, who saw great tactical use for Estienne's original concept for a 4 tonne armoured tractor with a crew of four, and able to drag a 7 tonne armoured sled carrying 20 infantrymen. The similarity to Swinton's original thinking is strong, and Estienne's tactical notion was that such an armoured force could 'sandwich' the occupants of the desired trench by pushing half its strength across the trench to isolate it and keep it under machine-gun fire.

Joffre appreciated the advantages of such a combination but was

The Germans' first tank design was notably unsuccessful, and the German army therefore pressed into service a number of British vehicles, often captured after suffering a mechanical breakdown and revised to Beutepanzerwagen IV standard with the 6pdr (57mm) guns replaced by 57mm Sokol cannon captured from the Russians and the machine-guns replaced by 0.312in (7.92mm) MG 08/15 machine-guns.

sufficiently astute to realize its impracticality. Ultimately, the French army reached the same conclusions as the British about the need for a tracked armoured vehicle that could cross barbed wire and knock out German machine-gun posts, and so open the way for the attacking infantry. Joffre therefore ordered Estienne to Paris where he was to liaise in the development of France's first tank with Eugene Brillie of the Schneider-Creusot company. This was the French licensee of the American Holt company, which had supplied one 45hp (33.6kW) and one 75hp (55.9kW) machine for trials purposes in May 1915. The basic design made extensive use of Holt components and practices, and was completed towards the end of 1915; on 31 January 1916 an order was placed for 400 of these tanks, to be designated Char d'Assaut 1 (CA 1) Schneider and delivered by November 1916. The Artillerie d'Assaut, as the French tank arm was named, was created in August 1916, and the first CA 1 Schneiders were delivered in September, just before Estienne was appointed commander of the tank arm.

The CA 1 Schneider was based on the Holt track system, which in this application was sprung by vertical coil springs and notable for its short overall length and very limited forward rise. The all-important trench-crossing and parapet-climbing capabilities were therefore wholly indifferent, and ground clearance was insufficient to give the tank useful performance under adverse conditions. The hull was basically rectangular, with a boat-hull nose section to aid parapet-climbing and reduce the tank's chances of embedding its nose in mud, and terminated at its front with a large serrated wire cutter. At the rear were a pair of upward-curving projections, designed to increase trench-crossing capability by increasing the tank's effective length. The CA 1 Schneider massed 13.50 tonnes under combat conditions, and was powered by a 55hp (41kW) Schneider petrol engine located at the front left of the vehicle (with the driver to its right), driving the tracks via a crash gearbox: steering was effected by clutches and brakes on the half shafts. As in the British Mk I, the petrol tank was located internally, to feed the engine by gravity. The CA 1 Schneider had a crew of six (an officer as commander/driver, an NCO as second-in-command, and four enlisted men in the form of a gunner, a loader and two machine-gunners), who entered and left the tank via large double doors in the rear. The armament was planned originally as one 37mm gun plus machine-guns, but the definitive fit comprised one short-barrel 75mm (2.95in) Schneider gun and two 8mm (0.315in) Hotchkiss machine-guns.

The CA 1 Schneider first saw action at Berry-au-Bac near the Chemin des Dames on 16 April 1917: of the 132 tanks committed, no fewer than 57 were destroyed and many others were damaged beyond economical repair. The primary culprits for this disaster were a combination of poor design and the

---

Schneider CA 1

DESIGNED for the assault role, namely the breakthrough of the Germans' trench lines so that the infantry and the cavalry could pour through the breech as undertake a deep exploitation into the enemy's rear areas to destroy artillery positions and supply lines, the Schneider CA 1 was not notably successful because of its poor trackwork. This was too short and too low to provide adequate trench-crossing and parapet-climbing capabilities, which were only 5ft 9in (1.75m) and 2ft 7in (0.787m) respectively despite the use of a lower hull with a boat-shaped 'stern' and 'bow', the latter with a tall wire breaker projecting upward and forward from the structure. The Schneider CA 1 was based on a maximum 11.5mm (0.45in) of armour, and its dimensions included a length of 20ft 8.75in (6.32m), width of 6ft 7in (2.05m) and height of 7ft 6.5in (2.30m). The tank had a crew of six, and its armament comprised one 2.95in (75mm) gun with 90 rounds of ammunition in a right-hand side sponson, and two 0.315in (8mm) machine-guns with 4,000 rounds of ammunition. The Schneider CA 1 was powered by a 55hp (41kW) Schneider petrol engine, and this was sufficient for a speed of 4.6mph (7.5km/h) on roads.

Germans' special 'K' bullet with its tungsten carbide core, which could penetrate the French armour without undue difficulty. The poor design concerned mainly the dismal ventilation and the location of the fuel tankage next to the machine-guns. After several tanks had blown up, the CA 1 Schneider was dubbed the 'mobile crematorium', an epithet that was slow to disappear even after the internal tankage had been replaced by two armoured external tanks; ventilation was also improved, but remained a problem under certain conditions. Protection was enhanced by the addition of rudimentary spaced armour over the most vulnerable areas.

Development and production of the CA 1 Schneider had bypassed the French army's normal vehicle procurement executive, the Service Technique Automobile (STA), which was sufficiently piqued to instigate the design and construction of another battle tank. This was the Char d'Assaut Saint Chamond, designed by Colonel Rimailho and ordered from the Compagnie des Forges et Acieries de la Marine et Homecourt (FAMH) at Saint Chamond. The first prototype was completed in February 1916, and two months later the STA ordered 400 of the type. Like the CA 1 Schneider, the CA Saint Chamond was based on the Holt sprung tractor system, although in this application with the track length increased by about 0.3m (0.98ft). This was clearly a basic improvement over the trackwork of the CA 1 Schneider, but was totally offset by the superimposition of an extraordinarily long hull: the result was cross-country performance still worse than that of the CA 1, with the tendency to ditch, even on slightly undulating ground; in terms of performance in front-line conditions, this translated into abysmally poor trench-crossing and parapet-climbing capabilities.

Two unusual features of the CA Saint Chamond were its provision for a unique rear driving position and its use of electric drive for the tracks. The Crochat-Collardeau electric generator was driven by a 90hp (67.1kW) Panhard petrol engine, and current was supplied to the electric motor attached to each track's drive sprocket. Differential powering of the tracks provided considerable agility within the limitations imposed by the hull, and

Built in very large numbers during World War I for the French and several of their allies, and maintained in production after the war in many variants for the French and a number of export customers, the Renault FT 17 was the first successful light tank developed anywhere in the world, and was a simple yet effective and reliable vehicle with a two-man crew and an armament of one cannon or one machine-gun. This is an FT 17 in service with a unit of the US Army during the Argonne fighting of 1917.

despite a combat weight of 22.00 tonnes the CA Saint Chamond had useful performance. The primary disadvantage of the electric drive system was its weight, which added to the mobility problems engendered by the long hull, which terminated at its forward end in a well-sloped glacis plate above an angled-back vee-shaped lower surface designed to help the tank ride over earth banks .

The CA Saint Chamond possessed a crew of eight including the driver and commander, who each had a small cupola at the front of the vehicle; access to the vehicle was provided by a door in each side plus another in the tail plate. The armament comprised one 75mm (2.95in) Saint Chamond TR commercial gun (first 165 vehicles) or one 75mm (2.95in) Modèle 1897 gun (last 235 vehicles), and four 8mm (0.315in) Hotchkiss machine-guns. The main gun was located in a limited-traverse mounting in the glacis plate, and the machine-guns were placed one in the bow (on the lower right-hand side), one in the tail plate, and one on each side of the hull. Deliveries of the CA Saint Chamond began in late 1916, and the type was first used in action in May 1917 at Moule de Laffaulx. In this first engagement, the limitations of the design became all too apparent: of 16 CA Saint Chamonds committed, 15 ditched in the first line of German trenches. Further action confirmed the need for modifications, which included: increasing the armour thickness against the effect of the German 'K' anti-tank bullet, a raised forward section of the hull, the elimination of the commander's cupola, the replacement of the original flat roof with a pitched roof so that grenades would roll off, and the use of wider tracks. These measures improved the tank's capabilities,

Weighing 6.7 tons, the FT 17 light tank had its driver in the forward lower part of the hull and its commander/gunner in the revolving turret. The vehicle was 16ft 5in (5.0m) long with the optional tail that increased its lower-hull length and thus its trench-crossing capability, 5ft 8.5in (1.74m) wide and 7ft 0.25in (2.14m) high, and was powered by a 35hp (26kW) Renault petrol engine for a speed of 4.8mph (7.7km/h). The armament illustrated here is a 0.315in (8mm) Hotchkiss machine-gun, for which 4,800 rounds of ammunition were supplied, and the alternative installation was one 37mm cannon for which 237 rounds of ammunition were supplied.

but nothing could be done about the basic design flaw in the vehicle's configuration, and from May 1918, when the final deliveries were made; the type was stripped of its main gun and used for supply tasks as the Char Saint Chamond de Ravitaillement.

Both the French chars d'assaut were perhaps ahead of their British contemporaries in gun calibre and in locating this single weapon in a central mounting, but the French designers had been too impressed with the cross-country capabilities of the Holt tractor to realize that a long track length combined with a large forward rise were essential elements for adequate trench performance. The two French tanks were thus little more than incidentals to the French army's war effort, although they did play an important part in the development of 'tank consciousness' and in the evolution of tank tactics and organization. However, the most important French tank of World War I was an altogether different machine, the Renault FT light tank, the designation indicating Faible Tonnage (light weight). The concept stemmed from Estienne's desire for a lightweight partner to his CA 1: the heavy tank would crush barbed wire and deal with the German strongpoints, and the lightweight machine would accompany the attacking infantry to suppress any surviving pockets of German resistance and develop the exploitation phase of any breakthrough.

Yet again, Estienne bypassed the normal channels of procurement, and in October 1917 went straight to Joffre with his scheme for 1,000 examples of a 4.00 tonne light tank carrying one 8mm (0.315in) machine-gun or a smaller number carrying one 37mm gun in a 360-degree traverse turret, armoured against small-arms fire, and possessing a maximum speed of

The FT 17 and its successors were comparatively cheap to build and possessed the advantages of useful manoeuvrability and considerable agility. Another advantage was the revolving turret, although this was limited in its utility by its ability to carry only one man, who had to double as the commander and gunner. Even so, the advanced nature of the FT series was reflected in the type's retention in service by several nations right into the opening part of World War II, some 25 years after the type had been designed.

The Dilemma of Turret Size

WITH the development of the turret on the Renault FT series, tank designers first encountered a problem that still remains, namely the optimum size of the turret. In essence, the answer to this dilemma is that there is no complete solution other than the fact that the designer must arrive at a judicious compromise. On the one hand, a large turret allows the incorporation of a larger and therefore more destructive and longer-ranged gun, allows the addition of the extra equipment that is inevitably required during the tank's operational life, and offers better working conditions for a larger and therefore tactically superior crew, which under ideal conditions can include a commander who controls the operation of the vehicle and looks for targets, a gunner and a separate loader. On the other hand, a large turret is more visible to the enemy and therefore more vulnerable, is heavier and therefore tends to destabilize the tank as well as degrade performance on the power of a given engine, and is also more expensive to produce in terms of material and man hours required. The designer therefore has to consider all these factors and arrive at a design that offers the blend of protection, gun size, crew size and working volume that best satisfies the requirements of his country's army.

12km/h (7.5mph). Estienne also proposed, in a very far-sighted manner, that a number of the machines should be completed with wireless equipment to allow communication between commanders and their mobile forces. Despite considerable resistance from some parts of the French war ministry, Estienne's notion found sufficient favour to secure authorization of prototype production after a mock-up had been completed at the end of 1916. The first prototypes appeared in February and March 1917, and immediately displayed excellent qualities in trials at the Champlieu camp. An initial order for 150 FTs was placed on 22 February 1917, but at the insistence of General Henri Pétain, the French commander-in-chief, the order was increased to 3,500 vehicles for delivery by the end of 1918, and additional orders increased the planned production run to more than double this figure. It was clear that Renault could not handle the orders on its own, and this important programme soon involved Belleville, Berliet, Delaunay, Renault and SOMUA as manufacturers, with a large number of other companies (including some in the United Kingdom) as subcontractors.

The FT was an unusual but interesting and successful tank in its technical and tactical features. Technically, the tank lacked a conventional chassis but was rather a monocoque of riveted armour plate, a box-like structure to which were attached the major internal and external components, terminating at the tail in an upswept plate that increased the effective length of the vehicle as an aid to trench crossing. The hull accommodated the driver at the front, the turret in the centre, and the combined engine and transmission assembly at the rear. The turret, surmounted at its rear by a mushroom-shaped observation cupola, was the world's first to offer 360-degree traverse. The engine was a 35hp (26.1kW) Renault petrol unit, and drove the tracks by means of a crash gearbox, with a clutch-and-brake system used for steering.

The first production tanks were completed in September 1917, but the whole programme was hampered by shortages of the special cast steel turret and by arguments within the army about the precise nature of the armament to be fitted. By the end of the year, Renault had delivered only 83 examples of the initial variant, which was designated the Char Mitrailleuse Renault FT 17 and was first used in combat on 31 May 1918 in the Forêt de Retz. The turret problem proved insoluble in the short term, and after the delivery of some pre-production vehicles with cast turrets, the producers designed their own eight-sided turrets of riveted plate construction, allowing larger-scale production from mid-1918 for the delivery of 3,177 tanks before the Armistice, against orders that currently totalled 7,820 including 3,940 from Renault. When the cast turret began to arrive in useful numbers it was installed on a version generally designated FT 18. The FT 17

Above: The LK.II was the German equivalent of the Medium Tank in British service, but was somewhat more heavily armed with a single 57mm gun in the front face of the fixed barbette above the hull rear. The vehicle was built only in small numbers, and was based on the chassis and axles of the Daimler car.

and FT 18 remained in service until the opening stages of World War II (1939-45), and were also exported in large numbers.

Such was the mainstream of French tank development in World War I, although a few experimental types were tested, including the Char 1, developed in two forms as a char de rupture (breakthrough tank) for the planned 1919 offensives and most importantly as the precursor of the Char 2C discussed below.

Given the dominant role played by German armour in the first half of World War II, it is interesting to note that Germany was not an outstanding tank operator in World War I. This cautious approach to the tank was not for lack of encouragement, for many army officers and civilians had advocated the development of tracked armoured vehicles. In was only after the British introduction of the tank as an operational weapon, however, that a major effort was launched towards the creation of a German tank superior in all significant capabilities to the British tank. Initial contracts were placed in

November 1916. Herr Steiner, the German representative of the Holt company, was appointed as adviser on the tracks, and the initial specification called for a Gelandespanzerwagen (all-terrain armoured machine) weighing 30.00 tonnes, powered by a 100hp (74.6kW) engine and armed with two guns (one in the front and the other in the rear) plus flank-mounted machine-guns or, in unarmed form, a payload of 4.00 tonnes.

The specification was hopelessly unrealistic, and failed to take into account the geography of front-line terrain. The Germans had to make an enormous technical effort in their attempt to catch up with the British, but like the French they made a large mistake in relying on the existing Holt track system as the core of their new vehicle, regardless of the fact that it lacked the cross-country capabilities required for parapet climbing and trench crossing. Working with Steiner, who was primarily tasked with the much-lengthened Holt track system, Josef Vollmer designed a massive machine, accommodating a crew of 18, that first ran in prototype form in April 1917. A wooden mock-up of the definitive version was inspected by the German general staff representatives in May 1917, and the design was accepted for production as the Sturmpanzerwagen A7V. The prototypes were thoroughly tested during the summer, and provided striking evidence of the design's failings, particularly in the tracks, and in the cooling system for the two 100hp (74.6kW) Daimler petrol engines that were located in the centre of the vehicle under the driver and commander. It was a practical but heavy drive system, decidedly lacking in power for a vehicle weighing 32.51 tonnes laden. This led to limited engine life and to overheating under all but the best of road conditions.

Slow and very unwieldy, the A7V was the only German heavy tank to enter production and service in World War I. The type had a large 18-man crew drawn from several branches of the German army, and this made the effective integration of the crew all but impossible. The tank's primary armament was a 57mm Sokol gun of which large numbers had been captured from the Russians, and a secondary armament of six 0.312in (7.92mm) MG 08/15 machine-guns was scattered round the sides of the large and highly vulnerable hull.

The Legacy of World War I

To most of the officers who reached senior rank during the war and remained in service after it, World War I was regarded as something of a military oddity that would, for reasons that they were unable to explain, not recur. Thus, in the opinion of these officers, never again would there be the conditions of trench warfare that required heavy tanks for assault purposes and light tanks for the exploitation of the breeches effected by these heavy tanks. The inevitable result of this thinking meant that there was little real demand for the retention of a tank arm after the war, or for the considerable expense of developing and producing more advanced tanks, especially of the heavy type for which no real role was foreseen. This woolly-headed belief in a return to the type of mobile warfare that hadt been seen as the norm in the second half of the 19th century, but which was now rendered impossible by the advent of barbed wire, the machine-gun and fast-firing artillery, was gladly seized upon by treasury departments desperate to reduce the scale of military spending in the 1920s, and led to the virtual end of tank development during this period. More advanced thinkers appreciated the potential of the tank, however, but these were generally more junior or middle-ranking officers whose opinions were usuallu condemned as having been tainted by the virtual heresy of armoured warfare.

The tracks lacked significant rise at their forward ends, limiting the A7V's parapet-climbing capability, while their short lengths provided only a disappointing trench-crossing ability. The low ground clearance also meant that the tank bellied on all but the levellest of hard surfaces; its performance on soft ground was poorer still. In short, therefore, the A7V had been designed as an armoured fort to co-operate with the infantry, but the German designers had neglected the aspect of mobility. The main armament, located in the bow plate, was a 57mm Sokol cannon from captured stocks, while the secondary armament comprised six 7.92mm (0.31in) MG08 machine-guns located as two in each side and two in the rear. The large crew was drawn from three separate army branches rather than from a homogeneous tank corps: the driver and two mechanics were engineers, the two men on the 57mm gun were artillerymen, and the commander and 12 machine-gunners were infantrymen.

The first vehicle was delivered in September 1917, the first fully-armoured example following in October. Daimler of Berlin was responsible for manufacture, the armour supplied by Krupp in Essen and from Steffens & Noelle in Berlin. There was considerable variation in the quality and nature of the armour plate supplied, some A7Vs having a hull made of a few large plates, but most having hulls in which smaller plates were riveted together (splash being a particular problem with these). There were still a large number of difficulties with the type, but the German general staff decided that it could wait no longer for improvements, and ordered 100 A7Vs on 1 December 1917, with delivery to be completed by the time of the great Spring offensives planned for 1918. Daimler, on the other hand, thought that a delivery rate of five per month was more practical, and only 35 or less machines had been delivered by the time of the Armistice. The type was first used operationally in the Battle of St Quentin in March 1918, and proved to be of little use for any task other than boosting the morale of the German infantry.

The only other countries to develop tanks to the hardware stage during World War I were Italy and the United States, which made determined efforts but achieved little success. The conditions in which the Italians were fighting the Austro-Hungarians were totally unlike those of the Western Front and therefore were not relevant to the armoured concept developed by the British and French. Neither the Italian nor the American types reached operational service in World War I.

Troubled Development

THE world's new tank arms had to ensure their survival, and secure emancipation from their positions subordinate to one of the armies' other arms. It was to be a difficult task occupying the 1920s and most of the 1930s. To the politicians, the tank could embody the concept of 'an engine of war' and thus smacked too strongly of militarism; to the economists, the tank represented a high level of development cost, followed by high production and operating costs; and to the professional heads of the world's most important armies the tank was an unessential embarrassment. The more far-sighted were content to see the retention of the tank in small numbers as an adjunct of the infantry (medium tank) and the cavalry (light tank), while the majority of soldiers wished to return to the pre-1914 pattern in which they had trained and gained most experience of practical soldiering. As a young arm, the tank service of most countries had attracted relatively junior officers with an interest in the mechanization that was becoming important in the period up to World War I, but without 'entrenched' attitudes to military operations. These men were able and eloquent, but had generally risen only into the lower levels of field rank, and were therefore able to achieve little but keep up a constant but carefully-controlled stream of propaganda to keep their tank arm alive pending the day it could prove itself.

Development of the tank in the period immediately following World War I was hindered by political, economic and social antipathy, and it was left to more far-sighted men to press ahead on shoestring budgets. One result was the Morris-Martel Tankette designed under the supervision of Major Sir Gifford Le.Q. Martel on the basis of commercial components supplied by the Morris company, which also undertook the construction of these prototype vehicles. This is the Two-Man Tankette of 1926, which was a half-tracked type with rear steering wheels.

The British squandered the technical and tactical lead they had established in World War I by a programme of parsimony so extreme that it could well have proved disastrous. Yet the British tank arm was saved by the twin efforts of men working solely within the professional confines of the army (middle-ranking officers such as P. Hobart, C. Q. Martel and Ernest Swinton), and a smaller number of men such as Colonel J.F.C. Fuller and Captain B. H. Liddell Hart, working mainly on the outside of the army framework to develop and promote their theories of armoured warfare.

Within the army, the middle-ranking advocates of armoured warfare worked to convince their largely sceptical superiors that the era of fully-mechanized warfare had arrived, and that the cornerstone of this new type of warfare was the tank. The army protagonists promoted the concept of the tank as embodying the primary virtues of firepower, protection and mobility in a package of unrivalled versatility; and at the same time they urged that the army opened its mind to the possibility of merging the new weapon with a new set of tactical doctrines whose absence would negate all the advantages of a tank force.

This accorded with the role played by Fuller and Liddell Hart, who were concerned not only with the practicalities of armoured warfare with present and future weapons, but with the 'ideal' of armoured warfare, and therefore the course in which the long-term development of tanks should be directed. At the core of the thinking of both Fuller and Liddell Hart was the concept that the tank was a new weapon, perhaps presaged in other weapons, but in its post-World War I form a weapon different from those of the infantry, cavalry and artillery, and as such requiring the formulation of a new set of tactical precepts.

Fuller was the tactical thinker par excellence, and his ideas stemmed directly from the British experience at Cambrai and Amiens: if it made full use of its mobility, the tank was unstoppable, giving its operating country

Seen coming to grief during its trials, the Fiat 3000 was the Italian-built development of the Renault FT with the engine mounted lower and transversely in the rear part of the hull. The original variant was the Fiat 3000 Modello 1921 with an armament of two machine-guns, but the vehicle seen here is the Fiat 3000 Modello 1930 (or Fiat 3000B) with a more powerful engine, exhaust silencers, a 37mm gun and a large vision cupola for the commander/gunner. The type was built in moderately large numbers for Italy, was exported to Albania, Ethiopia and Latvia, and was evaluated but not adopted by Denmark, Greece and Spain.

The DD (Duplex Drive) system was the British-developed method for creating an amphibious tank out of a conventional tank (here an M4 Sherman) without affecting its primary capabilities. The addition of a propeller provided propulsion on the water, and buoyancy was created by the addition of a folding canvas screen attached in a watertight fashion to the hull and erected only when waterborne operation was contemplated. The screen was lowered once the tank had reached land, thereby restoring the vehicle to full tank capability. The canvas screen could be discarded as the situation permitted.

the ability to strike at will against different points in the enemy's line; this would force the enemy onto the defensive and dilute his strength to the point that he would find it impossible to counter the tank attack and consequent breakthrough at the offensive's chosen point. The threat thus posed to the enemy's lines of communication would in turn force the enemy to retreat, the accumulation of such retreats leading inevitably to the enemy's defeat. Fuller was the great advocate of the 'all-tank' school of thinking, which averred that the evolution of the tank had rendered obsolete all other combat arms: cavalry had been rendered manifestly obsolete by the advent of mechanization, infantry was required merely to garrison that which the tanks had captured, and artillery should be replaced by special versions of tanks – fitted with large-calibre ordnances (self-propelled artillery) yet able to match the tank force for speed and mobility. In this last concept Fuller went too far, and in the process so threatened (or appeared to threaten) the established arms that they coalesced to frustrate Fuller's notions. In the long term, therefore, Fuller had a partially counterproductive effect on the development of the British tank arm when he moved out of the province of tactics into the more difficult intellectual and moral terrain of operational doctrine.

Working from the same basis of operational experience as Fuller, Liddell Hart transferred more easily from tactics into the field of operations and strategy, which were based on exploitation of the tank's speed (mobility) combined with its shock effect (firepower and protection). The key to Liddell Hart's concept was tactical and operational surprise: the initial offensive could be a hammer blow by massed armour into and through the enemy's front line, followed by an unrelenting exploitation in which the key was outright speed. Tanks must therefore be organized to push straight through the opposition or, if the opposition was too strong, to bypass and isolate it for elimination by the follow-up forces. By maintaining its impetus, Liddell Hart demonstrated, the tank force could punch through to the enemy's rear areas on a narrow front and then fan out in an 'expanding torrent' that would prevent the enemy's reserves from moving up in effective support: and then by destroying, capturing or incapacitating his command and logistic centres, the tank force would crush the enemy's capability to sustain the defence. It is worth noting here that Liddell Hart appreciated the full potential of the aeroplane for a battlefield role. Fuller had rightly realized the value of the aeroplane for reconnaissance and communication, but Liddell Hart recognized that the aeroplane was the ideal substitute for artillery in his 'expanding torrent', possessing greater mobility than the tank and having the three-dimensional agility to negate the effect of the enemy's anti-aircraft artillery while delivering attacks of great accuracy.

Liddell Hart's concept was remarkably far-sighted, but was not accepted in his own country as anything but an idealized picture of future warfare. This was a reaction with immense consequences.

The most important successes gained by the tank advocates were in the development of new vehicles, which possessed far greater mobility than their World War I predecessors in terms of agility, speed and range. The development programme was severely limited by lack of financial resources, and evolved via two main streams, namely the one- or two-man tankettes from Morris-Martel and Crossley-Martel, and the two- or three-man light tanks from Carden-Loyd and Vickers.

The tankette concept was forced on countries unable or unwilling to fund the development of larger and more capable vehicles, and was a conceptual dead-end, unimportant except as the precursor of the light tank.

The first practical light tank design was the Carden-Loyd Mk VII, a two-man vehicle that appeared in 1929 for evaluation as the A4E1. Although evolved from the earlier Carden-Loyd vehicles, the Mk VII provided striking proof of the pace of armoured vehicle development in the later 1920s, for it was a machine markedly superior to its predecessors in all respects. The armament was still a single 0.303in (7.7mm) Vickers machine-gun, but this was located in an exceptionally trim turret with bevelled edges on its top to reduce its silhouette. More notable, perhaps, was the increase in performance generated by the new running gear and more powerful engine.

Perpetuation of an Obsolete Doctrine

In the aftermath of World War I, Germany was prohibited from the possession and/or the development of tanks, and none of her allies of the defeated Central Powers had started work on such vehicles. Of the victorious Allies, the USA's tank-building industry was its its earliest infancy, the British, French and Italians were financially exhausted, and Russia (now the USSR after the Soviet Revolution of 1917) had yet to start on the design and production of tanks. It was France and the United Kingdom that were the only major powers capable of large-scale development of more advanced tanks. This was denied to them by a combination of financial retrenchment, moral and industrial exhaustion, and combined political and public antipathy to the concept of war and the weapons necessary for it. In the circumstances it was inevitable that tank development, such as it was, would be concentrated on small, and therefore cheap, vehicles designed to explore potentials and to keep alive the concept of armoured warfare. The resulting tankettes and light tanks inherited the mantle of World War I's medium tank in the 'cavalry' role, while tank designers and advocates pressed for the development of heavier tanks that inevitably came to be regarded as ideal for the 'infantry' role in two forms as the medium tank for the support task and the heavy tank for the breakthrough task. As funds for the development and procurement of these heavier tanks were made available in the late 1920s and early 1930s, the lighter tanks were retained in service rather than being discarded, and thus there emerged armoured forces based on two widely differing types of tank. The fallacy of this concept would be revealed only by World War II, which showed that the bulk of the armoured force should comprise multi-role battle tanks with good firepower, protection and mobility, with the balance comprising light tanks for the reconnaissance role with modest firepower and protection but very good mobility.

The former comprised four large road wheels in leafsprung pairs connected by an external girder, and the latter a 59hp (44kW) Meadows petrol engine: the result was a maximum speed of 35mph (56km/h) for this 2.54 tonne vehicle. Trials confirmed the overall suitability of the A4E1, which was developed for small-scale production as the Carden-Loyd/Vickers Light Tank Mk VIII, and accepted as the British army's first light tank in 1930 under the designation Light Tank Mk I. The running gear was revised and the new 58hp (43kW) Meadows EPT petrol engine provided a maximum speed of 30mph (48.3km/h) in a vehicle that weighed 4.88 tonnes.

The family directly evolved from the Carden-Loyd Mk VII ended with the Light Tank Mk III and Light Tank Mk IV. The Mk III entered service in 1933 as a Mk II with its superstructure lengthened to the rear, and the Mk IV series was produced in 1934 with a monocoque chassis to which components were directly attached.

By this time, the Royal Tank Corps had amassed a considerable volume of experimental and operational data with its first series of light tanks. Generally, it was satisfied that the light tank had a valuable role to play, although operational experience was limited to parts of the world where there was no effective opposition. However, while the monocoque hull, powerplant and running gear of the Mk IV still had value, the vehicle was limited in operational capacity by its one-man turret and its single machine-gun. An important step was thus taken with the 1935 adoption of the Light Tank Mk V. This was another Vickers-Armstrongs product, and was in practical terms the hull of the Mk IV with an enlarged fighting compartment surmounted by a new two-man turret. This was the first such unit fitted on a light tank, and for ease of traverse was mounted on a ball race: the armament comprised two Vickers machine-guns, one of 0.303in (7.7mm) and the other of 0.5in (12.7mm) calibre, and the turret was surmounted by a commander's cupola.

The Light Tank Mk VI entered service in 1936, and with it came the end of development by Vickers-Armstrongs on the basis of the Carden-Loyd Mk VII. The Mk VI was modelled closely on the Mk V, but with a longer hull

The Tank Mk IV was an effective weapon against barbed wire and machine gun strongpoints, and possessed the ability to traverse rough terrain and trench lines at modest speed. Even so, such behemoths could become bogged down, and in such circumstances the unditching beam carried on the top of the hull could be attached by chains to the tracks and thus brought forward, down and round to the underside of the trackwork to provide considerably greater traction for unditching purposes.

Lack of Operational Experience

PART of the problem with the develoment of tanks in the period between the two world wars was the operational vacuum in which the designers and operators lived. In the absence of major conflicts, at least up to the time of the outbreak of the Spanish Civil War in 1936, tank protagonists were forced to rely on their own conceptual thinking and on lessons that might be gleaned from the limited use of tanks in smaller wars such as the Gran Chaco War (1932-35) between Bolivia and Paraguay. These were hardly front-rank military nations even by South American standards, and the war was fought bitterly but inefficiently with tactical methods that resembled those of World War I and helped persuade those who followed such matters that the static nature of trench warfare was still relevant. The one occasion in which tanks were used, albeit in modest numbers, was in the Battle of Ayala (July 1933). Here the Bolivians attacked with three Vickers Six-Ton Tanks and two Carden Loyd tankettes, which operated in the support role: of the Six-Ton Tanks, one was finally knocked out by artillery fire, another by mechanical problems, and the third after an armour-piercing bullet had jammed its turret, and of the tankettes one was knocked out early in the engagement and the other was turned over in a trench. Two of the Six-Ton Tanks were repaired and committed again on the following day, but were withdrawn after all six crew members had been wounded by armour spall and bullet splash. The larger Six-Ton Tank was deemed to have been moderately successful, but the consensus was that the artillery shell and the armour-piercing bullet had the measure of the tank.

and the turret increased in length rearwards to allow the installation of a radio set. The type was mechanically reliable and cheap to produce, a combination that prompted large-scale orders: indeed, during the first month of World War II in September 1939, the British army fielded about 1,000 examples of the Mk VI family. Given the army's lack of recent combat experience against a high-quality enemy, these modest vehicles were used extensively in Europe, the Middle East and North Africa, and suffered heavy losses because of their lack of offensive and defensive capabilities.

The final pair of British three-man light tanks were both Vickers-Armstrongs designs: the Light Tank Mk VII Tetrarch of 1938 and its successor the Light Tank Mk VIII Harry Hopkins of 1941. The two types were built only in small numbers, and were similar in concept, being based on four independently-sprung road wheels of which the rear units served as drive sprockets and the front units as idlers; the steering was unusual, sharp turns were acheived by the standard skid occasioned by braking of the inside track, but gentle turns were effected by pivoting of the road wheels to curve the tracks. The Mk VII was armed with a 2pdr (40mm) main gun plus co-axial 7.92mm (0.31in) Besa machine-gun in a trim turret. The Mk VII had little practical application in World War II, its only real use being the provision of armoured support for airborne forces after their arrival in specially designed General Aircraft Hamilcar gliders. The type was also used in small numbers as the Tetrarch Infantry Close Support (ICS) with a 3in (76.2mm) howitzer instead of a 2pdr (40mm) turret gun.

The Mk VIII was intended to overcome the Mk VII's vulnerability by the adoption of armour that was both thicker and of superior ballistic shape: this increased weight to 8.64 tonnes, and Mk VIII production amounted to 100 machines, but these were never issued for service.

Such was the mainstream of British light tank development in the period between the two world wars. It is worth noting that, in addition to its Carden-Loyd derivatives for the British army, Vickers-Armstrongs also developed and produced two private-venture series of light tanks that enjoyed considerable export success. The first of these was the six-ton Tank Mk E powered by an 87hp (64.8kW) Armstrong-Siddeley engine. The second series was similar to the Light Tank Mk IV, although fitted with a bewildering array of armaments.

Further up the weight scale was the medium tank, for which the light tank provided reconnaissance and support: thus while the light tank was the inheritor of the World War I medium tank's mantle, the medium tank succeeded the (battle) tank of World War I. Initial British efforts in the period after World War I were the Medium Tank Mk D, continuing the effort already well under way in the war, and the Light Infantry Tank. The latter was again the work of Colonel P. Johnson of the government's Tank Design Department, and similar to the Mk D although smaller and lighter: its role was machine-gun support of infantry assaults, but work was ended in 1923 when the Tank Design Department was closed down as part of the government's financial retrenchment programme.

By this time, Vickers-Armstrongs had been invited to join the medium tank development programme, and its first design in this important field was the five-man Vickers Tank, produced in Nos 1 and 2 variants during 1921 and 1922. The overall configuration was akin to that of the Medium Tank Mk B, but the Vickers Tank sported a roof-mounted domed turret surmounted by a commander's cupola, and was the first British armoured fighting vehicle with its main armament in a 360-degree traverse turret. In the No.1 variant, the turret accommodated three 0.303in (7.7mm) Hotchkiss machine-guns in ball mountings, and in the No.2, one 3pdr (47mm) gun and four Hotchkiss machine-guns including one for anti-aircraft fire.

The Vickers Tank was mechanically unreliable, but experience with this type was invaluable for the company, and its next design was one of extreme importance in the evolution of tank design: the new vehicle was the world's first fast tank, allowing the type's use in the manoeuvres that validated the tactical and operational concepts of Fuller and Liddell Hart. The tank's body was positioned above the tracks so that adequate armament could be located in a revolving turret without loss of fields of fire, and reduction of length and weight allowed higher performance on the same power as earlier tanks. Designed in 1922 as the first British tank of genuine post-war concept, the five-man Light Tank Mk I was redesignated the Vickers Medium Tank Mk I after the army's decision to buy the Carden-Loyd/Vickers Mk VIII (the Light Tank Mk I). The 11.94 tonne Medium Tank Mk I entered service in 1924, and in its various forms was built to a total of about 160 machines that formed the mainstay of the Royal Tank Corps in the later 1920s and early 1930s, and remained in service until the period just before World War II. The Mk I was the first British service tank to have a 360-degree traverse turret and geared elevation for the main armament, and is also notable for the high speed made possible by sprung suspension. The tank had a box-like hull in which the driver was located at the front of the vehicle next to the engine, and the other four crew members were located in the fighting compartment and turret to deal with command, operation of the radio, and the handling of the armament. However, there were advanced and obsolescent features: the powerful 3pdr (47mm) Mk 1 L/31.4 main gun, was partnered by the

The Vickers Medium Tank Mk III of 1928 combined old and new features. The semi-rhomboidal trackwork with large mud chutes made for good mobility under adverse conditions, the large turret allowed the incorporation of both radio and wireless telegraphy equipment for better and more flexible control in battle, and a separate commander's cupola was installed over the turret for improved visibility in battle. The armament comprised a 3pdr (47mm) main gun and co-axial 0.303in (7.7mm) machine-gun in the main turret, and single 0.303in (7.7mm) machine-guns in each of the two subsidiary turrets located ahead and to each side of the main turret. The crew was seven men, and 'production' was limited to three 16 ton development vehicles.

obsolescent secondary armament of four 0.303in (7.7mm) Hotchkiss guns in the turret plus a pair of Vickers guns of the same calibre in the hull sides.

Given the type's longevity of service, it is not surprising that the basic machine was developed into variants with a number of mechanical and operational improvements.

In 1925 Vickers-Armstrongs introduced the improved Medium Tank Mk II with thicker armour (at the penalty of a weight increase to 13.415 tonnes), and the longer 3pdr (47mm) Mk 2 L/40.05 gun with a higher muzzle velocity for better armour penetration; the driver was located farther forward for improved fields of vision, and the suspension was protected by skirt armour. This basic type was also developed in a number of improved forms.

During 1925 as the Medium Tank Mk II was entering service, Vickers-

Armstrongs was involved in the design of the Vickers Independent Tank that pioneered a number of advanced features and had a profound effect on tank design outside the United Kingdom. This tank inaugurated the new British system of tank nomenclature, being officially designated the A1E1, and was delivered to the Mechanical Warfare Experimental Establishment in 1926 for exhaustive trials, but which did not lead to a production order because of financial restrictions rather than any major problem with the tank itself. Among the Independent Tank's more advanced features were intercommunication among the eight-man crew by throat-mounted laryngaphone, a long wheelbase with the hull built up between the suspension assemblies, hydraulically powered controls and wheel steering for all but the sharpest turns. For its time, the Independent was a massive machine, weighing 32.01 tonnes and measuring 25.42ft (7.75m) in overall length. Power was provided by a 398hp (267kW) Armstrong-Siddeley petrol engine. Most unusual (and widely copied in Germany and the USSR) was the armament system, which comprised one main turret with four subsidiary turrets clustered round it. The main turret was fitted with a 3pdr (47mm) Mk 2 gun and incorporated a cupola for the commander, whose laryngaphone communication with all other crew members was

Despite its limitations, the Medium Tank Mk A, otherwise known as the Whippet, was well suited to the exploitation of the breakthroughs secured by the British army after the Battle of Amiens during August 1918, roaming ahead of the advancing infantry to keep the beaten Germans off balance and cut their lines of communication.

complemented by a pointer system to indicate targets to any of the turrets. The subsidiary turrets were each fitted with a single 0.303in (7.7mm) Vickers machine-gun.

Until the early 1930s the British had remained confident that they had the right 'mix' of armoured vehicles in the form of the light tank for reconnaissance, and the medium tank for independent mobile operations and support of the infantry. The realization of the need for a rapid re-armament programme, forced by Germany's growing strength and belligerence, drove the army towards the decision that it could best cater for the independent mobile and infantry support roles with different tank types. As a result, the medium tank was supplanted by the cruiser tank for mobile operations and by the infantry tank for support operations.

The first cruiser tank was the A9, otherwise known as the Cruiser Tank Mk I, and designed by Sir John Carden of Vickers-Armstrongs in 1934. The type entered small-scale production in 1937 as a 12.70 tonne vehicle with a crew of six, a 150hp (112kW) AEC Type 179 petrol engine, and an armament of one 2pdr (40mm) gun plus one 0.303in (7.7mm) machine-gun in the power-traversed main turret and one Vickers machine-gun in each of two subsidiary turrets. The use of a 2pdr (40mm) gun in place of the previous standard 3pdr (47mm) weapon may appear a retrograde step, but was in fact a highly sensible move, as the smaller-calibre weapon had far higher muzzle velocity and armour-penetrating capability than the larger weapon.

Production of the A9 amounted to only 125 vehicles, and the type remained in service up to 1941, seeing operational use in France and North Africa.

At much the same time, Vickers-Armstrongs undertook design of the A10 as an infantry tank, using the A9 as its basis but increasing the armour thickness: the additional armour took the form of plates attached to the hull (the first use of appliqué armour on a British tank), and increased the weight of the vehicle to 13.97 tonnes. The engine remained unaltered, and this led to a reduction in maximum speed. The subsidiary turrets of the A9 were not retained, and in 1940 the Vickers co-axial machine-gun was replaced by a 7.92mm (0.31in) Besa, a weapon of the same type which was sometimes added in the nose in place of some of the ammunition stowage. By the time the A10 was ready for production it was clear that the time lacked adequate protection for the infantry role, and the type was classified as the Heavy Cruiser Tank Mk II.

A turning point in British tank design was heralded in 1936 by the decision to develop new cruiser tanks on the basis of the suspension system devised in the USA by J. Walter Christie and already adopted with a high degree of success by the Soviets for their BT series. The Christie suspension used large-diameter road wheels attached to swinging arms supported by long coil springs: this gave the individual road wheels great vertical movement. In its basic form the Christie suspension system provided for high speed over adverse terrain, but considerable work had to be undertaken to turn the system into a battleworthy suspension for the new cruiser tanks. The result was incorporated in the A13. The prototype was completed in 1937 and performed excellently as a result of the Christie suspension combined with a high power-to-weight ratio: the A13 was powered by a 340hp (253.5kW) derivative of the World War I Liberty aero engine and weighed 14.43 tonnes, which resulted in a high maximum speed combined with unprecedented cross-country performance. Only moderate armour and armament were provided, as the tank was intended to rely on performance and agility for its protection. Armament comprised a turret-mounted 2pdr (40mm) gun and a 0.303in (7.7mm) Vickers co-axial machine-gun. The reduction in the number of machine-guns did not seriously affect

the tank's ability to defend itself against infantry attack, and had the advantage of allowing a reduction in crew to just four men.

Deliveries of the resultant Cruiser Tank Mk III started in December 1938 and were completed in 1939, when the improved Cruiser Tank Mk IV began to appear. The Mk III was used in France during 1940 and in North Africa during 1941, but proved a failure because of its wholly inadequate armour.

It was this failing that the Mk IV (also designated the A13 Mk II) was designed to overcome through the provision of additional armour in its more important areas. Even so, the Mk IV was decidedly under-armoured by the standards of its contemporaries. The Mk IVA introduced a 7.92mm (0.31in) Besa co-axial machine-gun in place of the original Vickers, and also featured a Wilson combined gearchange and steering gearbox. As with the Mk III, range was too limited for effective independent operations, and the angular design of the box-like hull and Vee-sided turret provided many shot traps.

The next British cruiser tank was the A13 Mk III, otherwise known as the Cruiser Tank Mk V Covenanter. This resulted from official dissatisfaction with the speed of an unsuccessful type, the A14 prototype, and the LMS Railway Co. was asked to develop a cruiser tank with considerably better speed than the 29.97 tonne A14. The Covenanter was essentially the A13 Mk II with a purpose-designed 300hp (224kW) Meadows engine, thicker armour, and a low-silhouette turret designed to optimize ballistic protection by increasing armour angles. The tank was a combat vehicle of some potential, and production eventually totalled 1,771, but the type was beset by intractable problems with engine cooling and, despite evolution through four marks in an effort to overcome these difficulties, was never used in combat. The Covenanter nevertheless proved invaluable as a training tank. The standard armament was one 2pdr (40mm) gun and one 7.92mm (0.31in) Besa co-axial machine-gun, but the close-support variant of each of the four marks was fitted with a 3in (76.2mm) howitzer.

The A12 Infantry Tank Mk II, otherwise known as the Matilda II, epitomises all that was right and wrong with British tank design in the late 1930s. Ordered 'off the drawing board' in 1937 as a breakthrough tank and built to the extent of 2,987 vehicles between 1940 and 1943, the 26.5 ton Matilda II was reliable but slow, was very well protected with armour ranging in thickness between 20 and 78mm (0.79 and 3.07in) for virtual invulnerability to German anti-tanks guns of the period except at very short ranges, but was also very decidedly underarmed with a 2pdr (40mm) main gun supported by just one 0.303in (7.7mm) machine-gun.

In the mid-1930s the British realized that, whereas previous tanks had been fitted with the 14mm (0.55in) armour deemed sufficient to stop the anti-tank projectiles fired by small arms, the advent of specialist anti-tank guns in calibres of 37mm or greater posed a new threat. The cruiser tank was evolved as successor to the medium tank in its mobile independent role, but with only modest armour as it was to rely on agility and speed for its main protection. The infantry support role demanded a new type of tank with considerably greater armour protection, as agility and speed would not be appropriate to the operational task envisaged. The division of the medium tank role into the cruiser and infantry roles coincided with the appointment of General Sir Hugh Elles (commander of the Tank Corps in World War I) to the position of Master General of the Ordnance. Elles thus had considerable operational experience of the direct infantry support role, and despite the technical and financial objections of many interested parties, Elles was insistent that a new breed of infantry tank should be evolved: the primary requirements being invulnerability to the fire of 37mm anti-tank guns, and good performance in adverse conditions.

The design task was entrusted to Sir John Carden of Vickers-Armstrongs, but the predetermined unit cost of each vehicle dictated that Carden had to work to very fine limits. The resulting A11, or Infantry Tank Mk I Matilda, gave every indication of having been designed down to a price rather than up to a specification, yet it managed to achieve one of the concept's primary requirements, through the use of armour varying in thickness between 10mm and 60mm (0.39in and 2.36in). It is acknowledged that, up to the end of 1940, the A11 was among the world's most heavily armoured tanks, and this helped to reduce losses. This was fortunate perhaps, for the A11 was not adequately planned in terms of armament, the limiting price having forced Carden to design a small vehicle whose two-man crew dictated the use of a one-man cast turret armed with a single 0.303in (7.7mm) Vickers machine-gun, later altered to one 0.5in (12.7mm) Vickers machine-gun in a move that increased firepower but further cramped the already uncomfortable turret.

Even as the A11 was starting prototype trials in 1936, the War Office was concluding that the infantry tank should not only be well protected but also sufficiently well armed to deal with enemy positions as well as infantry. A cursory examination showed that the A11 could not be evolved in such a fashion, and it was decided to limit A11 production to 139 machines that would serve as interim types pending the arrival of a superior infantry tank. This was the A12, otherwise known as the Infantry Tank Mk II Matilda II and designed by the Tank Design Department of the Mechanisation Board on the basis of the 1932 A7 prototype, using the same running gear (strengthened for greater weights) and powerplant of two 87hp (64.9kW) AEC diesels driving through a Wilson gearbox. The design was ordered straight into production, and for lack of tank-experienced companies with the capability for making large armour castings, manufacture was entrusted to the Vulcan Foundry of Warrington, with other companies brought in as the programme expanded. Most of the castings for the heavy hull and turret armour were produced by Vulcan, which was responsible for final assembly. Production eventually amounted to 2,987 vehicles, and the risky decision to order the type 'off the drawing board' was validated by generally successful capabilities from the beginning of trials. The 26.97 tonne Matilda II was of course heavier than its predecessor, but this allowed the carriage of a four-man crew and the installation of a larger turret accommodating a 2pdr (40mm) gun and one co-axial machine-gun. Improvement during World War II was undertaken wherever possible, resulting in the Mk IIA* Matilda III

Tank Warfare on the Outer Mongolian Frontier

ALTHOUGH they were the main producers and exponents of the tank in the 1920s, France and the UK could not pursue their chosen course on the basis of lessons learned in contemporary armoured warfare, for such warfare was virtually nonexistent in that decade. The same problem affected American, British and French developments in the 1930s, but did not apply to countries such as Germany, Italy, Japan and, more importantly, the USSR. Japan used her tanks in the somewhat atypical fighting of her campaign to conquer China, but then in the late 1930s came up against the altogether more formidable Soviet armoured capability in two major campaigns along the river borders between the Japanese-occupied Korea and Siberia in 1938, and the Japanese puppet state of Manchukuo (Manchuria) and the Soviet client state of Mongolia in 1939. The more serious of the clashes took place between May and September 1939 along the Khalkin Gol river near Nomonhan, and here the Japanese made the mistake of using their light and medium tanks to support conventional infantry assaults, which were severely handled by the Soviet infantry with generally superior artillery support. Meanwhile the Soviets had been massing a major armoured force in the form of the 4th Tank, 6th Tank, 7th Mechanised, 8th Mechanised, 9th Mechanised and 11th Tank Brigades. (The mechanised brigade was a tank brigade with a battalion of motorised infantry.) This force was allocated to the Soviet left and right wings which, once the Japanese had been pinned by the advance of the Soviet centre, were to sweep round the flanks and take the Japanese in the rear after cutting their lines of communication. The plan was devised by the local commander, General Georgi Zhukov, and introduced the type of tactic used with overwhelming success in World War II. This success was presaged by its triumph in the Nomonhan fighting, in which the Soviets virtually destroyed the Japanese 6th Army in the type of combined-arms fighting that received little attention at the time but was to portend with some exactitude the nature of armoured warfare used in World War II.

with two 95hp (70.8kW) Leyland diesels, the Matilda III CS with a 3in (76.2mm) howitzer, the Matilda IV with mechanical improvements over the Matilda III, the Matilda IV CS with mechanical improvements over the Matilda III CS, and the Matilda V which was identical to the Matilda IV but with a directly-operated pneumatic gearbox.

So far as the situation in 1939 was concerned, one must conclude that official indifference and lack of funding were responsible for the parlous condition of British tank strength: the light reconnaissance tank was available in useful numbers but was obsolete, the medium tank was outdated, the cruiser tank was unproven in concept and was too lightly armed and armoured, and the infantry tank was also unproven and was too slow. This dangerous situation was compounded by lack of adequate design and manufacturing capabilities, and by the failure of the higher authorities to grasp the nettle of German tank superiority when this became evident.

Like the United Kingdom, France was faced with problems of how to develop its armoured force after World War I, especially as financial resources were in short supply and the role of the tank was in question. Most production orders were cancelled at the end of World War I, and much of the in-service tank fleet was in fact unserviceable because of the cumulative mechanical defects of designs that had been rushed into production too hastily. General J. E. Estienne, meanwhile, set to work on the tactical and operational roles of an independent tank arm evolved from the Artillerie d'Assaut of World War I, using a derivative of the Char 1 as its first major vehicle. However, the Artillerie d'Assaut was disestablished in 1920 and the tank arm subordinated to the infantry, tank units thereafter serving as components of infantry formations.

Opposite top: Variously known as the Renault Type ZT or AMR 35, this vehicle was a light tank developed from the Type VM with slightly lower overall performance and reduced versatility offset by better crew comfort and improved vision devices. The type was of bolted construction, and was generally armed with one 0.295 or 0.512in (7.5 or 13.2mm) machine-gun or, as illustrated here, a 25mm Hotchkiss anti-tank gun. Production totalled 200 vehicles.

Opposite bottom: Also known as the Renault Type VM or AMR 33, this vehicle was a light tank of bolted construction and was optimised for the reconnaissance role with an armament limited to one 0.295in (7.5mm) machine-gun carried in the revolving turret mounted centrally above the superstructure above the rear of the hull.

The main heavy battle tank of the French army at the time of the German invasion of May 1940, the Char B1-bis was a 32-ton development of the Char B1, itself a development of the Char B prototype. The type was built from 1937 by Renault. The four-man type was costly to produce but was considered to be highly effective with cast and bolted steel armour varying in thickness between 20 and 60mm (0.79 and 2.26in), and an armament that comprised one 2.95in (75mm) gun with 74 rounds in the hull front, one 47mm gun with 50 rounds in the revolving turret, and two 0.295in (7.5mm) machine-guns with 5,100 rounds. The Char B1-bis was 21ft 4.75in (6.52m) long, 8ft 2.5in (8.2m) wide and 9ft 2in (2.79m) high, and its 180hp (134kW) Renault petrol engine provided a speed of 17.4mph (28km/h).

In 1921 the French formulated their first programme for tank development, calling for a char de rupture (breakthrough tank) and a char de bataille (battle tank), the latter to succeed the Renault FT in the infantry support role. Under the auspices of the Section Technique des Chars de Combat, this programme produced one breakthrough tank (the Forges et Chantiers de la Mediterranée 2C of which only a few were built) and five possible battle tanks from Delaunay-Belleville, FAMH (Saint Chamond), FCM and Renault/Schneider.

After assessment of the five char de bataille proposals and examination of four mock-ups in 1924, the Section Technique des Chars de Combat ordered single Char B prototypes from FAMH, FCM and Renault/Schneider in 1927. The specification had called for a weight of 15.00 tonnes, a crew of four, and a main armament of one hull-mounted 47mm or 75mm (2.95in) gun. The prototypes appeared between 1929 and 1931, with a weight of 25.00 tonnes, a hull-mounted 75mm (2.95in) SA 35 main gun, and a secondary armament of four 7.5mm (0.295in) Chatellerault machine-guns (two fixed in the forward hull and two flexible in the turret). After exhaustive trials in the 1932 French army manoeuvres, the Char B was ordered into production in a revised form as the Char B1. This entered service in 1935 with a main gun fixed in traverse (the whole tank having to be slewed to bring the gun to bear on the target) but movable in elevation, while the turret accommodated one 37mm gun plus a 7.5mm (0.295in) co-axial machine-gun. Only 36 Chars B1 had been produced before the considerably revised Char B1-bis was introduced with heavier armour, revised armament, and a more powerful

The logic behind the design of the Char B series was the creation of a tank that would be virtually invulnerable to enemy anti-tank fire as a result of its heavy armour, and able to serve as a breakthrough tank with the fire of its general-purpose main gun located in the hull front, with the smaller turreted gun providing capability against tanks and strongpoints. The concept had some merit, but resulted in a tall and somewhat cumbersome vehicle whose main gun was fixed in azimuth so that the whole vehicle had to be slewed to bring the gun to bear on its intended target.

The PzKpfw I was a light reconnaissance tank with machine-gun armament, and was intended not so much as a combat vehicle but as a type on which German industry could cut its teeth and the new German armoured arm could develop some experience in the operation and use of armoured fighting vehicles.

engine. The Char B1-bis weighed 30.00 tonnes, was armoured more extensively with bolted-together castings to the maximum of 40mm (1.575in), had a revised turret accommodating one 47mm gun and one 7.5mm (0.295in) co-axial machine-gun, and featured a 250hp rather than a 180hp (186kw rather than 134kW) Renault petrol engine: production amounted to 365 vehicles by June 1940.

The last development of this potent armoured fighting vehicle, still one of the most formidable weapons of its type in 1940, was the Char B1-ter of which five were produced. This featured a 310hp (231kW) Renault engine, a maximum armour thickness of 70mm (2.76in), a main gun provided with limited traverse, and a crew increased to five by inclusion of a mechanic in the enlarged fighting compartment.

In 1926 the French produced a new tank programme providing for three tank types, in the form of the char léger (light tank) with one 37mm gun and 7.5mm (0.295in) machine-guns, the char de bataille with a main gun of 47mm calibre or more, and the char lourd (heavy tank) with thicker armour than the char de bataille. Little money was available to the French army during this period, most available resources being devoted to the fixed defences of the 'Maginot Line', and the programme was generally unsuccessful. The main results were the Renault Chars NC1 and NC2 improved versions of the FT, which secured export orders but failed to win French approval. Considerable development of tactical ideas followed in the early 1930s as the infantry and cavalry expanded their thinking about the nature and employment of armour, but France's sole armoured warfare visionary, Colonel Charles de Gaulle, fell into political oblivion after the publication of his *Vers l'Armée de Métier*. This called for a professional rather than a conscript army of mechanized shock troops centred on armoured divisions, and ran counter to all the tenets of France's pacifist government.

In 1931 the infantry organized its armoured force by type of equipment in service or under development, all such infantry vehicles being designated

chars: the chars légers (light tanks) were the Renault R-35 and R-40, FCM-36 and Hotchkiss H-35; the new category chars moyens (medium tanks) were the Renault D1 and D2, and AMX-38; the chars de bataille were the Char B series; and the chars lourds were the Char 2C series. The cavalry followed suit in 1932 with a wider-ranging classification of auto-mitrailleuses (machine-gun cars) that included wheeled armoured cars: the AMD (Auto-Mitrailleuse de Decouverte) category comprised long-range armoured cars; the AMR (Auto-Mitrailleuse de Reconnaissance) category comprised cross-country light reconnaissance tanks with machine-gun armament, such as the Renault Type VM and Type ZT; the AMC (Auto-Mitrailleuse de Combat) category comprised gun-armed tanks such as the Renault Type YR and Type ACG1; and the char de cavalerie category added in 1935 covered heavier gun-armed tanks such as the Hotchkiss H-35 and H-38/39, and the SOMUA S-35 and S-40.

Compared with their German opponents in 1940, the PzKpfw I and II, the French tanks had generally superior armament and protection, but were let down tactically by their two-man crews, their use in small non-homogeneous units, and (with the exception of the R-35 series) their comparatively small numbers.

The chars moyens were intended as medium-weight infantry support tanks. The most important of these was the Char D produced by Renault in

Whereas the PzKpfw I was limited to an armament of two 0.312in (7.92mm) machine-guns, the PzKpfw II was somewhat better armed with a 20mm cannon and co-axial 0.312in (7.92mm) machine-gun. The vehicle had a crew of three, and is seen here in its first definitive model, the PzKpfw II Ausf C of which some 2,000 were produced mainly for the development of the German armoured force but also for limited operational use in the Spanish Civil War and, as a result of tank shortages, in the first part of World War II. This model differed from its predecessors mainly in the adoption of revised running gear with five road wheels and elliptical springs on each side for improved cross-country mobility.

response to the 1926 new tank programme and based mechanically on the Renault NC 1 (NC27) light tank that secured export rather than domestic sales. The first prototype appeared in 1931, and production of 160 tanks was undertaken between 1932 and 1935. The key to this model was the use of a two-man cast turret (one of the first such units in French service) on a riveted hull with skirt armour to protect the running gear. The crew of three was well provided with vision devices, and a radio with a distinctive triangular antenna was standard. The Char D1A was armed with a 37mm main gun and a co-axial 7.5mm (0.295in) machine-gun, plus a fixed machine-gun of the same calibre fired by the driver, and at a weight of 12.00 tonnes the tank had a maximum speed of 18km/h (11.2mph) on its 65hp (48.5kW) Renault petrol engine.

Technically one of the best tanks fielded by any of the combatants at the beginning of World War II was the SOMUA S-35, which was a char de cavalerie. This was the world's first tank with all-cast hull and turret construction, and was arguably one of the ablest armoured fighting vehicles of its day anywhere in the world. The turret was an electrically traversed unit with a maximum thickness of 56mm (2.2in), and was identical with the turret used by the Char B1-bis and Char D2: the main armament was the 47mm SA 35 gun, and the secondary armament comprised a 7.5mm (0.295in) co-axial machine-gun in an unusual mounting that allowed limited traverse independent of the turret; there was also provision for mounting a second 7.5mm (0.295in) machine-gun on the commander's cupola for anti-aircraft defence. The S-35 had a combat weight of 20.05 tonnes, was powered by a 190hp (142kW) SOMUA petrol engine, and had a crew of three.

Of all the countries which were to become the Allied powers of World War II, that making the greatest strides in the development of armoured fighting vehicles in the interwar period was the USSR. As in other countries, ideas for armoured fighting vehicles abounded in the years before and during World War I, considerable numbers of armoured cars being placed in service and some development towards genuine tanks being undertaken as supplies of British and French tanks were received. But the first tanks were not produced until after World War I, by which time revolution had replaced Tsarist Russia with the Soviet state. The Soviets were impressed

The Char D2 was a French medium tank intended for the infantry support role. Deliveries of the type from the Renault production line began in 1934, although production was limited to just 50 vehicles produced by 1936 as the new SOMUA S-35 offered better all-round capabilities. The three-man Char D2 weighed 18.5 tons, was powered by a 150hp (112kW) Renault petrol engine for a speed of 14mph (22.5km/h), and was armed with one 47mm gun in the revolving turret supplemented by one 0.295in (7.5mm) machine-gun that could be a co-axial weapon or a fixed weapon in the nose plate

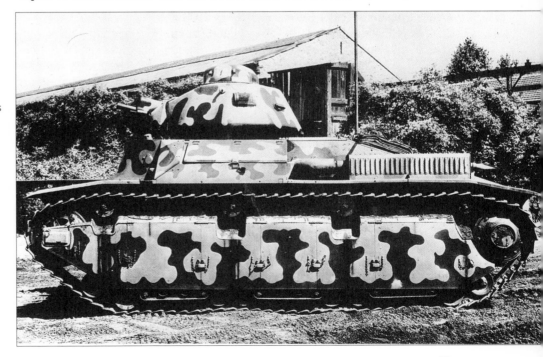

Strv m/37 was the Swedish designation for a Czechoslovak light tank, the CKD/Praga AH-IV-Sv. Weighing 4.5 tons and armed with two machine-guns in the revolving turret, the two-man Strv m/37 was produced to the extent of 50 vehicles assembled in Sweden by Jungner from components delivered in crates from Czechoslovakia.

Designed as successor to the T-32 heavy tank, the T-35 remains the classic example of the multi-turret tank in the period leading up to World War II. Weighing 45 tons and manned by a crew of 10, the tank was powered by a 500hp (373kW) petrol engine for a speed of 18mph (29km/h), and its armament was centred on a main turret and four subsidiary turrets. The main turret carried a 3in (7.62mm) gun, the right-hand forward and left-hand rear auxiliary turrets each carried a 37mm (later 45mm) gun, and the left-hand forward and right-hand rear auxiliary turrets carried two of the six 0.3in (7.62mm) machine-guns that constituted the tertiary armament. Production was limited to about 30 tanks, some of which were later stripped of some if not all of their auxiliary turrets in an effort to improve performance and agility.

with the capabilities of tanks, and avidly seized those left behind by the departing 'interventionist' Allied forces. The Renault FT suited their requirements admirably, and in 1919 they ordered an FT 'clone' into indigenous production as the Krasno-Sormova (KS), which was identical to the FT in exterior detail but featured an American gearbox and 45hp (33.6kW) Fiat engine. Production was limited by lack of Soviet industrial capacity, and this also affected the thinking towards the development of other tanks. In direct violation of the 1919 Treaty of Versailles, the Soviet authorities readily agreed to the establishment of a secret German tank centre at Kazan in the USSR, and thereby kept abreast of German developments. Combined with overt purchases of the best of foreign tanks, this allowed the Soviets to keep their tactical and technical thinking fully appraised on modern developments without the risks and costs of an indigenous tank programme. A wholly-Soviet design was also attempted, but nothing came of this effort before the Central Armoured Force Command was dissolved in the early 1920s and further design was entrusted to the War Department Tank Bureau created in 1923.

The consolidation of the Soviet state continued steadily during the 1920s, allowing the promulgation of the wide-ranging First Five-Year Plan in 1927. This included the notion of mechanizing the Red Army, and also of developing tanks in all categories now deemed essential for a modern army. The plan called for each division to have a supporting group of tanks, and the MS series was considered to be an adequate basis for the first generation. These vehicles included the T-17 one-man tankette, the T-19 and T-20 two-man light tanks, the T-21 two-man light tank, the T-23 two-man tankette, the T-24 three-man medium tank and the TG five-man heavy tank. All were failures for a variety of reasons, with lack of mechanical reliability proving the single most significant factor. The 25.40 tonne TG heavy tank was of notably advanced concept with low silhouette, armament of one 75mm (2.95 in) gun and four machine-guns, and a 300hp (224kW) petrol engine.

That the Soviets had appreciated the possible failure of this programme is given credence by the contemporary purchase of much of Vickers-Armstrongs' tank range, including Carden-Loyd tankettes, Six-Ton Light Tanks, Medium Tank Mk IIs, Carden-Loyd A4E11 amphibious tanks and tractors. A thorough technical and tactical analysis of these vehicles provided the Soviets with the starting point for a new generation of designs based on sound principles rather than the assumptions of World War I. Just as significantly, however, several of these British tanks were passed to the Germans for evaluation at Kazan, and it is not surprising therefore that Carden-Loyd and Vickers-Armstrongs features appeared in several German tank designs of the early 1930s. It is also worth noting that at this time the Soviets were astute enough to investigate tank developments of other sorts, exemplified by their purchase of licences for German BMW engines and the US Christie suspension in 1930.

Evaluation of these tanks and associated components was completed at the beginning of 1931, and the decision was made to cancel production of the T-19 to T-24 series in favour of the Six-Ton Light Tank (as the T-26 light tank), the Carden-Loyd Mk VI (as the T-27 tankette), and the Carden-Loyd A4E11 (as the T-37 and improved T-38 light amphibious tanks). All were produced in large numbers and as several steadily improving variants, providing the Soviets with a first-rate introduction to modern design, manufacturing and operating principles. The Christie M1931 (T-3) medium tank was also accepted for production as the BT-1, the first variant of the BT (Bistrokhodny Tank, or fast tank) series, although the Soviets were mindful that this was not a tank well suited to operational use. Modest production was undertaken, however, to provide Soviet designers with a data base of experience with the Christie suspension which, unlike the complete Christie tank, was clearly well suited to the nature and extent of the theatres likely to be forced on the Soviets in any future war.

Germany Enters the Scene

AFTER the Armistice of 11 November 1918, the German army's tank force was disbanded, and the Treaty of Versailles of June 1919 included, among its many provisions, a total ban on the development of tanks. Yet the German army was already well established on its programme of intelligence-gathering about foreign developments, clandestine evaluation of tank-capable components in Germany, and secret links with countries not unsympathetic to German liaison in the development of their own tank forces. In this last respect the Swedes were the Germans' most important 'allies' in the early 1920s, when the LK.II was readied for Swedish production and service as the Strv m/21 under the leadership of Vollmer and a German army team. As the 1920s progressed the Germans became increasingly involved with the Soviets, both parties thinking that a fair deal had been struck when the Germans were given use of the Kazan tank school as an experimental and proving ground, in return for technical information and training provided to the fledgling Soviet tank arm.

Between 1926 and 1929 the Germans broke the strictures of the Treaty of Versailles to produce a number of experimental tanks. These were commissioned in great secrecy from major engineering and arms companies as a means of evaluating trends in the design of armoured fighting vehicles, and also of regaining a manufacturing capability pending the day that Germany would move into the field as a major armoured force.

Accompanying this technical and manufacturing effort was a great deal of theoretical thinking about the operational and tactical employment of armour. By a paradox typical of military history, the Germans were well served by their lack of armour in this period: it left them without the entrenched thinking and existing hardware that inevitably accompanies the existence of in-service weapons, and opened the way for radical and professionally competent thought about the nature and employment of a future tank force. Coupled with a realistic analysis of the German army's performance in World War I, this paved the way for the adoption of the Blitzkrieg (lightning war) concept of operations, derived ultimately from the thinking of Fuller and Liddell Hart towards massive breakthroughs or bypassing of the enemy's major front-line assets by massed armour, with substantial air support as the first step in fast-moving operations into the enemy's rear areas.

While these tactical and operational concepts were still in their embryonic phases, the Germans were moving towards the creation of new hardware with a number of prototype vehicles such as the Leichte Traktor VK31 and Grosstraktor, so designated to convey the impression of an agricultural role and thus not contrary to the provisions of the Treaty of Versailles.

The German army began to plan its overt growth to world capability in 1932, and an accelerating implementation and augmentation of this plan followed the Nazis' rise to power. Plans had already been laid for the

The PzKpfw I was too poorly armed and armoured to be of usefull service with the German armoured divisions in the first part of World War II, but a number of the vehicles such as this PzKpfw I Ausf B were adapted as command tanks with additional radio equipment.

development of a tank force based on existing prototypes, but the recommendations of men such as Oberst Heinz Guderian for a massive force of comparatively light armour used in the Blitzkrieg concept of fast-moving operations found favour with the army's political masters, who recognized the military and propaganda value in a multitude of smaller vehicles that could be obtained for the same financial and industrial outlay as a considerably smaller number of heavier vehicles. In 1933, therefore, the German army started to plan a family of tactically interrelated armoured fighting vehicles for development over the next few years. However, the need to train large numbers of tank crews and support personnel, and the development of the appropriate tactical doctrines through practical training, coincided with political demands that Germany must be seen to be developing a tank force. The result was a requirement for a nominal 5 tonne light tank with a crew of two and an armament of two turret-mounted 7.92mm (0.31in) MG13 machine-guns. Designs were commissioned from Daimler-Benz, Henschel, Krupp, MAN and Rheinmetall for a light tank weighing between 4.00 and 7.00 tonnes; the Krupp LKA I design (with features of the Carden-Loyd Mk VI tankette in its running gear) was accepted and construction by Henschel of three LaS prototypes began in December 1933. The first mild-steel prototype was running by February

The first tank to enter production in Germany after World War I, the PzKpfw I was intended as little more than a training type on which the new Panzer divisions could begin to learn their trade. The vehicle illustrated here is a PzKpfw I Ausf A, which was the pre-production model produced to the extent of 100 vehicles in three subvariants for the evaluation of different suspensions and other details.

1934, and after successful trials, an initial production contract for 150 vehicles was placed in July 1934, later contracts raising the total to about 1,800. Of this number about 300 were of the initial PzKpfw I Ausf A model with four road wheels, and the remainder were of the more powerfully engined PzKpfw I Ausf B variant with five road wheels.

The PzKpfw I was the main vehicle used by the German tank force up to the beginning of World War II, and was largely responsible for the high quality of German tank tactics, maintenance and overall capability at the beginning of the war. The type was also used operationally in the Spanish Civil War (1936-39), and confirmed the tactical limitations imposed by a two-man crew and armament of only two machine-guns. The armour varied from 7mm to 13mm (0.28in to 0.51in) in thickness, which was confirmed as too thin for genuine operational capability. The total obsolescence of the design led to the PzKpfw I's retirement from front-line roles from 1941.

In 1934 it became clear that the German army's definitive PzKpfw III battle tanks and PzKpfw IV medium tanks would take longer to develop than anticipated, and it was decided to produce an interim type to succeed the PzKpfw I, which would offer superior operational qualities with a crew of three and an increased nominal weight of 10 tonnes. Designs and prototypes were tendered by Henschel, Krupp and MAN, that eventually selected for development as the LaS 100 being the MAN design with a 130hp (96.9kW) engine and a turret-mounted armament of one 20mm KWK 30 cannon and one 7.92mm (0.31in) MG13 co-axial machine-gun. Trials were undertaken with the pre-production LaS 100 a3 (PzKpfw II Ausf a3) and improved PzKpfw II Ausf b with thicker armour and a 140hp (104kW) Maybach HL 62 TR engine. Extensive trials were continued in this period, together with operational trials in the Spanish Civil War, and resulted in the 1937 arrival of the PzKpfw II Ausf C with a full-width superstructure, a revised turret, and completely remodelled suspension based on five larger-diameter road wheels with independent elliptical springing.

This led to the first service model, the 7.305 tonne PzKpfw II Ausf A with improved protective features but otherwise similar to the Ausf c. The PzKpfw II Ausf B introduced a slightly more powerful engine and revised tracks, while the PzKpfw II Ausf C was similar except for thicker frontal armour for a weight of 9.50 tonnes. Full-scale deliveries began in 1937, and such was the pace of production that 1,000 PzKpfw IIs were available for the Polish campaign that started World War II. The type was clearly as good as any light tank in the world in the late 1930s, but by the beginning of the 1940s the position was changing, and when the PzKpfw II was used in the Western campaigns of May and June 1940, it maintained an admirable reconnaissance capability but was a liability when forced to fight: even the frontal armour was too thin to stop the British 2pdr (40mm) shot, and the kWK 30 cannon projectile could not penetrate the armour of British and French medium tanks.

Development of the basic machine was still continuing, however, and in 1939 Daimler-Benz produced the PzKpfw II Ausf D and Ausf E variants with revised running gear, which utilised the Christie pattern with four large road wheels. Cross-country performance was inferior to that of the Ausf A to Ausf C variants, and in 1940 most surviving vehicles were converted to other roles.

The main stream of development therefore evolved from the Ausf C, resulting in the 1940 introduction of the PzKpfw II Ausf F with solid conical-hubbed rear idlers in place of the previous open spoked type, and frontal armour thickened by the addition of spaced appliqué plates to defeat the hollow-charge anti-tank warhead that was becoming increasingly lethal to battlefield tanks. Further evolution of the same basic theme resulted in the PzKpfw II Ausf G and Ausf J variants with a stowage box on the turret bustle and other detail modifications. Production of the PzKpfw II series continued into 1941, when the start of the war against the USSR proved beyond doubt that the type was obsolete.

The PzKpfw III was the most important German medium tank in the first part of World War II, and was planned as the backbone of the Panzer divisions' strength with heavier support provided by the PzKpfw IV. The type had a crew of five, and in its various main forms had a weight of approximately 20 tons. The very first tanks of this type were armed with a 37mm main gun and had coil spring suspension, although all later vehicles had heavier armament (a 50mm or later a 75mm gun) and torsion bar suspension. The illustration shows a PzKpfw III, here armed with a short 50mm gun that was later replaced by a longer weapon of the same calibre, involved in the fighting around Tobruk on the North African coast during 1942.

By 1935 the German designers and industrialists had gained sufficient experience with the PzKpfw I and II light tanks to embark upon the first of Germany's definitive battle tanks, the five-man PzKpfw III with a nominal weight of 15 tonnes. The German army's plan at this time was to field a force based on two main types, one a battle tank with a high-velocity anti-tank gun backed by machine-guns, and the other a medium tank with a medium-velocity gun backed by machine-guns and intended mainly for the support role; the battle tank became the PzKpfw III with a 37mm gun (later a 50mm gun), while the medium tank became the PzKpfw IV with a 75mm (2.95in) gun. The standard tank battalion had four companies, and it was planned that three of these would field the battle tank and the fourth would use the medium tank.

Development of the battle tank was undertaken with the cover designation ZW, and prototype orders were placed with Daimler-Benz, Krupp, MAN and Rheinmetall during 1936. The Inspectorate for Mechanized Troops wished the ZW to be fitted with a 50mm gun, but the Ordnance Department pointed out that the infantry's standard anti-tank gun was a 37mm weapon: a compromise announced that the type would carry the 37mm KWK L/45 gun but with a turret ring of adequate diameter to allow later substitution of the 50mm KWK 39 gun if tactical conditions altered. This was an extremely far-sighted move, and allowed the PzKpfw III to be retained as an effective weapon for about two years longer than would otherwise have been the case.

It proved impossible to design a battle tank down to the desired weight of 15 tonnes, so the upper limit was raised to the 24 tonne rating of Germany's

In a definitive form such as the Ausf F and G, the PzKpfw III was armed with an L/42 gun of 50mm calibre that was replaced in models such as the PzKpfw III Ausf J, L and M by an L/60 weapon of the same calibre. The PzKpfw III Ausf H, which was first produced in 1941 with the L/42 gun but later switched to the L/60 weapon, carried two 0.312in (7.92mm) machine-guns as its secondary armament, weighed 21.6 tonnes, was protected by armour varying in thickness between 30 and 80mm (1.18 and 3.15in), and possessed dimensions that included a length of 18ft 1in (5.52m), width of 9ft 8in (2.95m) and height of 9ft 8in (2.95m). The PzKpfw III Ausf H was powered by a 300hp (224kW) Maybach HL 120 TRM petrol engine for a maximum speed of 25mph (40km/h).

road bridges, and the selection battle settled down to a choice between Krupp and Daimler-Benz; the latter was selected for production of the PzKpfw III Ausf A after features of the Krupp MKA prototype had been incorporated into the design. In overall layout the PzKpfw III followed the pattern finalized in the PzKpfw I: the five men of the crew were favoured with considerable working space by comparison with contemporary tanks of the same basic type, and the driver had the useful advantage of a preselector gearbox: this required more maintenance than the crash gearbox used in most other tanks, but offered greater flexibility of operation in conjunction with the 230hp (171.5kW) Maybach HL 108 TR petrol engine. The sensible layout of the vehicle was echoed in the construction of high-grade chrome/molybdenum steel armour: the hull was a bolted-together assembly of three welded subassemblies (the lower hull, the forward upper hull and the rear upper hull), and the turret was another welded assembly. The armament rather let down the potential of the tank, being the 37mm KWK L/45 gun and three 7.92mm (0.31in) MG34 machine-guns (two co-axial with the main armament and the third in the bow).

The first production model (or perhaps the last pre-production model as only 440 were built) was the PzKpfw III Ausf E, which appeared in 1938 with the 320hp (239kW) Maybach HL 120 TR engine.

At about this time the Ordnance Department finally appreciated its short-sightedness in pressing for a 37mm main armament, and instructed Krupp to proceed with the design of a new turret to accommodate the 50mm KWK 39 gun. The development had not been completed, however, when the next variant of the tank III was being readied for production in early 1940 as the PzKpfw III Ausf F. This 20.30 tonne variant therefore had to retain the 37mm

The PzKpfw IV was conceived as the heavier partner to the PzKpfw III with a larger gun for the support rather than the anti-tank role, and in all its variants was delivered with a 2.95in (75mm) gun that was gradually increased in length and lethality as the PzKpfw IV superseded the PzKpfw III as the standard tank of the Panzer divisions. The PzKpfw IV had the distinction of remaining in production right through World War II.

gun, and its main improvements over the Ausf E comprised better ventilation, a stowage box on the turret and the HL 120 TRM engine rated at 300hp (224kW). The new main armament was still not ready when the PzKpfw III Ausf G was introduced later in 1940, so this variant also retained the 37mm main gun. It had the same weight and improvements as the Ausf F, but also featured a revised commander's cupola with improved protection for the vision ports.

All three of these variants were retrofitted with the new kWK L/42 gun as this became available, to the annoyance of Hitler who appreciated the pace of armoured warfare development and thus demanded the longer and more powerful kWK 39 L/60 gun of the same calibre. Development of the PzKpfw III continued after 1940, and details of the ultimate extension of the PzKpfw III's capabilities are discussed in the next chapter.

The last of Germany's main tanks with a pre-war pedigree was the PzKpfw IV, which possesses the distinction of being the only German tank to have remained in production right through World War II, with an overall total in excess of 8,500 examples. The type was planned at the same time as the PzKpfw III, and was essentially similar apart from its main armament, which was the 75mm (2.95in) kWK L/24 designed to provide the lighter PzKpfw III with high-explosive (HE) fire support.

The design was fixed at a weight not exceeding 24 tonnes, and prototype vehicles were ordered in 1934 under the cover designation BW, from Krupp as the VK2001(K), MAN as the VK2002(MAN) and Rheinmetall as the

Based on the Krupp VK.2001 prototype, the PzKpfw IV was numerically and tactically the most important tank fielded by the German forces in World War II. The type entered production as the PzKpfw IV Ausf A during 1937, and went through a number of forms with a 2.95in (75mm) gun of steadily increasing length, thicker and better disposed armour protection, uprated engines, and other enhanced operational features. Typical of the later variants was the longer gun (originally an L/43 weapon but later an L/48 ordnance) fitted with a muzzle brake for reduced recoil loads. Common to all variants was the trackwork, with four track-return rollers and eight small bogie wheels in pairs on each side.

VK2001(Rh). The Krupp submission was selected in 1936 for production after the incorporation of features from the Rheinmetall prototype, including the simpler running gear, on each side consisting of eight small road wheels in two-wheel bogies with leafsprings.

The crew was disposed in much the same way as in the PzKpfw III, but whereas the battle tank had a manually operated turret, that of the medium tank was traversed electrically. Before the PzKpfw IV entered large-scale production, a number of features were trialled in small pre-production batches, and it was only late in 1939 that the type entered full-scale production as the PzKpfw IV Ausf D, which differed from its predecessors primarily in general improvement of its protection. This indicated that the German army was now becoming seriously worried about the comparatively thin armour of its primary tanks, and this strengthening was continued with the PzKpfw IV Ausf E that was identical to the Ausf D in all but its improved protection and its new turret. The protective features included the thickening of the nose plate and, once a suitable machine-gun mounting had been evolved, the front plate; the turret protection was also improved by the addition of face-hardened panels, and spaced armour of various types was often added as a retrofit.

The Ausf E introduced the type of turret that remained standard on production vehicles for the rest of World War II. Some criticism had been levelled at the inadequate protection offered by the commander's cupola, and this was improved in the revised turret. The cupola was also moved forwards, allowing the installation of a smoothly curved back plate without the distinctive cut-out previously necessary to accommodate the rear of the cupola. Finally, the turret was fitted with an electrical ventilation fan, replacing the original ventilator flap. The PzKpfw IV went through later marks and developments, but these fall within the context of World War II and are therefore described in the next chapter.

Germany's design and industrial capabilities were severely tested by the virtually simultaneous development and production of four major service tanks, yet despite a prodigious effort, they could not satisfy the army's requirement in terms of volume and speed of production. To this extent, the army was fortunate that Hitler's territorial ambitions encompassed the overrunning of Czechoslovakia's rump in March 1939, after the ignominious British and French abandonment of the Czech Sudetenland to German demands in the Munich agreement of September 1938. The German army was able to absorb much of the Czech army's capable tank fleet, and the

During the German invasion and conquest of France in May and June 1940, the PzKpfw IV was used in its initial support role with a short 2.95in (75mm) gun firing an assortment of ammunition types including HE shell.

Czech production capabilities were completely at the disposal of the German war machine, which accepted two tanks of Czech design and manufacture, namely the CKD/Praga TNHP (otherwise LT-38) and Skoda LT-35 light tanks.

The spur for the development of the TNHP was the Czech army's reaction to a rapidly worsening European situation, by the creation in October 1937 of a committee to evaluate current Czech tank production capability and to recommend a new type of high-performance light tank to complement and later to supplant the Skoda LT-35, a 1935 type of exceptional performance but notable mechanical complexity.

The 8.00 tonne TNHP was the classic light tank of the period immediately before World War II, with a balanced blend of firepower, protection and mobility to optimize its capabilities in the twin roles of reconnaissance and support for the more powerfully armed medium tank. The weakest points of the design were the riveted construction (with the exception of the bolted-on upper surfaces to the superstructure) and the modest 37mm Skoda A7 gun. In layout the tank was conventional, with the driver in the forward compartment, the commander, gunner and loader/radio operator in the fighting compartment, and the powerplant in the rear compartment under a comparatively high rear decking. The turret was surmounted by a fixed cupola, and its weapons comprised one 37mm gun and one 7.92mm (0.31in) vz37 co-axial machine-gun; another vz37 machine-gun was located in the bow for operation by the driver. The engine was a 125hp (93.2kW) Praga EPA unit.

PzKpfw 35(t) was the German designation given to the Skoda S-IIa/T-II light tank after the occupation of Czechoslovakia in 1938. This advanced four-man light tank was armed with a 37mm main gun supported by two 0.312in (7.92mm) machine-guns, and was notable for the comparative spaciousness of its fighting compartment. Production was continued after the German occupation to provide the Panzer divisions with additional vehicles pending the delivery of larger numbers of German tanks.

When Czechoslovakia was occupied by Germany in 1939, the TNHP was just entering service with the Czech army and was taken into German service as the PzKpfw 38(t). Production was then continued against German plans for 40 such vehicles per month, ending only in 1942 after the production of 1,168 vehicles for the German army within an overall chassis production figure of 1,590. The Germans were concerned with the TNHP's comparatively light protection, and ordered increases in the basic protection to produce the 9.70 tonne TNHP-S, the suffix standing for Schwer (heavy). In many vehicles the German 37mm KWK L/45 gun was used in place of the Skoda L/47.8 weapon, and considerable revisions were made to the internal equipment to modify the vehicle to German standards. In the last 500 chassis, an uprated powerplant was installed in the form of the 150hp (112kW) EPA/AC engine.

The LT-35 (sometimes LTM-35) was designed by Skoda to satisfy operational requirements, such as rear drive to leave the fighting compartment uncluttered by transmission elements, a short engine to allow as much floor area as possible for the fighting compartment, a pneumatically-operated gearbox for transmission flexibility and ease of driving, pneumatically powered steering to permit the coverage of long distances without excessive driver fatigue, new running gear to ensure equal pressure on all road wheels, and duplication of all major accessories to increase system reliability in sustained operations. For its time the design was highly advanced, but suffered the consequences of its mechanical complexity in low serviceability. Nonetheless, the performance of the type in prototype trials was so impressive that at the end of 1935 the tank was ordered into production for the Czech army. The hull and turret were of riveted and bolted construction. The driver and bow gunner were located in the forward compartment, the latter to operate the 7.92mm

Inspired by the Soviet T-34 tank with its well-sloped armour and long-barrel gun, the PzKpfw V Panther was one of the classic tanks of World War II and may be credited with establishing the tank concept that was later adopted by the Western nations in the closing stages of World War II for the new generation of tanks that entered service in the late 1940s and early 1950s. The four-man Panther was notable for its good performance and agility as a result of the high power-to-weight ratio offered by its 650hp (485kW) petrol engine, the thickness and sloped nature of its armour, and the use of a long-barrel 2.95in (75mm) gun that provided excellent armour-penetration capability and which because of its twin-baffle muzzle brake, did not provide undue recoil forces.

55

(0.31in) bow machine-gun, and the commander/gunner and loader/radio operator were placed in the first 360-degree traverse turret to be installed on a Skoda tank. This turret, tactically limited by its two-man crew, was fitted with a fixed cupola, and was armed with a 37mm Skoda A3 L/40 semi-automatic gun and a 7.92mm (0.31in) co-axial machine-gun.

After German occupation of Czechoslovakia the LT-35 was taken into German service as the PzKpfw 35(t). The type continued to suffer reliability problems, and the Germans redesigned the tank's transmission and steering systems. From 1942, however, the type was phased out of front-line service for the less exacting but important role of mortar and artillery tractor.

After the rise of the Fascist party in Italy under Benito Mussolini, Italy increasingly swayed from its World War I alliance with France and the UK towards a political adherence to Germany, especially after the rise of the Nazi party in Germany. This consensus of right-wing political beliefs led to a formal alliance between Germany and Italy in May 1939. As noted above, Italy had perceived little utility for the tank in the context of its particular operational scenario in World War I, but nevertheless developed one important type (the limited-production Fiat 2000 heavy tank), improved on the Renault FT amongst others. With the end of World War I, Italian orders were immediately curtailed from 1,400 to a mere 100 examples of Italy's modified FT, the Fiat 3000. This served the Italian army well into the 1930s, and it was the late 1920s before serious consideration was given to a successor.

For a variety of economic, tactical and industrial reasons, Italy was drawn to the example of the Carden-Loyd Mk VI tankette, which offered useful if limited capabilities and also the possibility of large-scale production at modest cost by an automotive and armament industry with only small capacity for heavy engineering. The result was the CV (Carro Veloce, fast vehicle, or tankette) series, which began in 1929 with the CV.29, a vehicle

Italy was never able to match either the number or quality of the tanks produced by Germany in World War II, as evidenced by the fairly antiquated design of the Carro Armato M13/40 medium tank, which was based on riveted armour of inadequate thickness. Production amounted to 1,960 vehicles including a number completed to the standard illustrated here, namely the Semovente 40 da 75/18. This was a three-man self-propelled gun with a 2.95in (75mm) gun/howitzer in the front of the superstructure.

that was similar to the Mk VI and built only in small numbers (25 examples) as the precursor of an improved version of Italian origin, produced in prototype form as the CV.3 and, after evaluation in 1932 and 1933 with different running gear and water- or air-cooled machine-gun armament, was standardized for service as the CV.33 (alternatively the CV.3-33). The order was for 1,300 vehicles, of which 1,100 under the designation CV.33 Serie I were armed with a 6.5mm (0.26in) machine-gun, and the remaining 200, under the designation CV.33 Serie II, were armed with two 8mm (0.315in) machine-guns. Most Serie I tankettes were later brought up to Serie II standard, but this could not disguise the overall obsolescence of the type. Considerable development was undertaken on the basis of this simple vehicle. The CV.35 (sometimes designated CV.3-35) had a redesigned hull of bolted rather than riveted construction and slightly revised suspension, but was otherwise unaltered from the CV.33, while the L.38 of 1938 was a more ambitious updating of the basic concept with strengthened suspension, new tracks, improved vision devices, and an armament of one 13.2mm (0.52in) Breda machine-gun revised in 1940 to one 20mm Solothurn s13-1000 cannon. The 1938 system of nomenclature led to the redesignation of the CV.33 as the L.3-33 and of the CV.35 as the L.3-35 in the L-series of Leggero (light) tanks.

The CV.33 was intended primarily for security and reconnaissance duties in association with heavier tanks, but the nature of the Italian industrial machine dictated that when Italy entered World War II in June 1940, her armoured forces were still equipped with the L.3, which therefore had to be used for the type of combat role for which it was not designed and consequent losses were very high.

The replacement for the L.3 was the Fiat-Ansaldo L.6/40 light tank, of which 283 were ordered. The first prototype ran in 1940 and production began in 1941. The riveted turret, manned by the single commander/gunner, carried one Breda 20mm cannon and one 8mm

Japan's relative lack of industrial capacity combined with the nature of the war in China, which Japan launched in 1937 to gain a major empire on the Asian mainland, to persuade the Japanese army that it did not need advanced tanks. It was content, therefore, to retain obsolescent vehicles such as this two-man Tankette Type 94 that first appeared in 1934 with a welded and riveted hull carrying a turreted machine-gun of 0.303in (7.7mm) calibre.

57

(0.315in) co-axial machine-gun. The only other crew member was the driver who sat at the front of the 6.80 tonne vehicle, which was powered by a 70hp (52.2kW) SPA 180 petrol engine for a maximum speed of 42km/h (26.1mph).

Another stream of development from the Ansaldo light tank of 1935 resulted in the Carro Armato M.11/39, which was the first of the M-series of Medio (medium) tanks and destined to become Italy's most important tank of World War II. The design was started in 1936, and then pursued with considerable vigour after combat experience in the Spanish Civil War had revealed to the Italians the total inadequacy of the CV.35, in face of even moderate anti-tank capability. The first prototype was completed in 1937, and used running gear modelled on that of the CV.33/CV.35 series combined with the 105hp (78.3kW) SPA 8T diesel engine and armament layout of the 1935 light tank. The M.11/39 entered service in 1940, but an alarming loss rate revealed its concept to be obsolete.

The third of the Axis powers in World War II was Japan, which had fought on the Allied side in World War I but then fell under the sway of increasingly right-wing military administrations and drifted into the same political arena as Germany and Italy; in 1940 the three countries signed the German-Italian-Japanese Axis agreement, a 10-year mutual assistance pact. Japan was slow to enter the field of armoured warfare, and thereafter produced a number of vehicles that were adequate for her operations on the Asian mainland but were considerably inferior to their Western counterparts in overall capabilities.

The best of these vehicles was the Light Tank Type 95 (Ha-Go), without doubt the best tank produced and deployed in quantity by the Japanese in World War II. The prototype was built either by the Sagami Arsenal or Mitsubishi, and was extensively evaluated in Japan and under the operational conditions encountered in China before production was entrusted to Mitsubishi, which built about 1,250 examples from its own and subcontracted assemblies. The type entered service in 1935, and for its time was a capable machine and as good as any light tank in the world, the provision of an interior layer of asbestos proving useful in reducing interior heat and protecting the crew from injury as the tank moved at speed across country.

Otherwise known as the Ha-Go, the Light Tank Type 95 was the best vehicle of its category available to the Japanese in any numbers during World War II, and was a 7.4-ton vehicle with a crew of three, an armament of one 37mm gun and two 0.303in (7.7mm) machine-guns, and a 110hp (82kW) diesel engine for a speed of 25mph (40km/h).

The 7.40 tonne machine was based on a welded and riveted hull, with a forward compartment for the driver and a gunner, and had a 6.5mm (0.26in) bow machine-gun. Behind this was the turret, also of welded and riveted construction, which accommodated the commander who, in addition to his command responsibilities, had the task of loading, aiming and firing the 37mm Type 94 main gun. At the rear were the 120hp (89.5kW) Mitsubishi NVD 6120 diesel engine and transmission.

Operational use in Manchuria and China confirmed that better armament was desirable, and the 6.5mm (0.26in) bow machine-gun was replaced by a 7.7mm (0.303in) weapon, another 7.7mm machine-gun was added on the right-hand side of the turret rear for use by the already overworked commander/gunner, and the original Type 94 main gun was replaced by a Type 98 weapon of the same calibre but with higher muzzle velocity.

The Light Tank Type 95 proved moderately successful in campaigns such as that during late 1941 and early 1942 in which the Japanese overran Malaya and seized the fortress city of Singapore.

The Type 95 was a major improvement over the Japanese army's previous light tanks, but was soon involved in an intensive programme to produce improved variants. The first of these was the Light Tank Type 98-Ko (Ke-Ni) that entered production in 1942 for construction of perhaps 200 vehicles, although some sources suggest only 100. The Ke-Ni used a greater proportion of welding than the Ha-Go, was better armoured, and carried an armament comprising one 37mm Type 100 high-velocity gun and two 7.7mm (0.303in) machine-guns.

The Japanese viewed the medium tank as a battle tank with modest armour, good armament and only limited performance as a battlefield support weapon for the infantry. The best of these vehicles was the Medium Tank Type 97 (Chi-Ha), a four-man machine weighing 15.00 tonnes. In basic concept the Type 97 was a scaled-up version of the Light Tank Type 95 with a two-man turret, thicker armour and greater power to maintain performance despite the considerably greater weight. The hull was of riveted and welded construction, with the driver and gunner for the 7.7mm (0.303in) bow machine-gun in the forward compartment, the fighting compartment in the centre, and the engine and transmission in the rear compartment. The turret was surmounted by the commander's cupola, and its weapons comprised one 57mm Type 97 short-barreled tank gun and, in the rear face, one 7.7mm (0.303in) machine-gun. The turret provided 360-degree traverse, but the main gun had a second pair of trunnions allowing a maximum 10-degree traverse independently of the turret. The Type 97 entered service in 1938 and remained in major service until the end of World War II.

The Japanese were not unaware of the progress in tank tactics, however, and sensibly provided the Type 97 with a turret ring of greater diameter than required by the 57mm medium-velocity gun. This allowed for the later development of the Type 97 (Shinhoto Chi-Ha), which was essentially the hull of the Type 97 fitted with the turret of the Medium Tank Type 1 complete with its 47mm Type 1 long-barrel gun. This increased combat weight to 16.00 tonnes, but the longer gun provided a higher muzzle velocity and greater armour-penetration capability.

Blitzkrieg

THE last chapter described the main stream of tank development in the period between the two world wars. There had been some armoured conflict during this period, most notably between the Soviets and the Japanese in a number of border clashes in eastern Asia, and between the Nationalist and Republican forces in the Spanish Civil War, but these conflicts lacked the sustained intensity neccessary for any valuable long-term conclusions to be drawn. It was clear from these conflicts, however, that armour had a potentially decisive part to play if reliability could be improved, numbers increased and offensive power boosted. The two countries to recognize these implications were Germany and the USSR: Germany used the Spanish Civil War to validate the basic premises of its

The best-known German tank of World War II, the PzKpfw VI Tiger is revealed in this cutaway illustration, which highlights the central location of the large turret and the size of the rear-mounted engine. Notable features of this monumental tank were the thickness of the armour, which was not significantly sloped for additional ballistic protection, the massive nature of the very powerful 3.465in (88mm) gun, and the . relatively low power-to-weight ratio that rsulted in indifferent performance coupled with poor range owing to a relatively small fuel capacity.

new Blitzkrieg concept, and the USSR decided that its considerable capacity for tank design and production would be best used in development of a new generation of high-speed tanks with superb cross-country performance, hard-hitting main armament, good protection and reliability enhanced by the ruthless elimination of less essential items of equipment.

From late 1940, the mainstay of the German army's Panzer battalions were the PzKpfw III battle tank and the PzKpfw IV medium tank, as the PzKpfw I and II had become obsolescent and were relegated to secondary roles. The PzKpfw III was designed as the German army's standard battle tank, and entered its stride as a production weapon with the PzKpfw III Ausführung H, the main production variant in the period between late 1940 and the end of 1941. The first large-scale production variant, the PzKpfw III Ausf E, had been allocated for production to several companies with little experience in the manufacture of armoured fighting vehicles, and had suffered in terms of production quantity and quality because of the comparatively complex manufacturing techniques required. The PzKpfw III Ausf H incorporated features to ease mass production, the most important being new idlers and drive sprockets, and a transmission arrangement with a six-speed manual gearbox in place of the original 10-speed preselector box. As a result of combat experience in Poland and the Western campaign, extra protection was added in the form of bolt-on plates as well as a measure of spaced armour to defeat hollow-charge warheads. This boosted the PzKpfw III Ausf H's combat weight to 21.60 tonnes, and wider tracks were fitted to reduce ground pressure. The 300hp (224kW) Maybach HL 120 TRM petrol engine

PzKpfw VI Ausf E Tiger

THE only tank variant of the original Tiger model to enter production and service was the PzKpfw VI Ausf E, which was a heavy battle tank with a weight of 56.9 tonnes and a crew of five. This vehicle had a length of 27ft 9in (8.46m) with the gun trained directly ahead, a width of 12ft 3in (3.73m) and height of 9ft 6in (2.90m), and in its definitive later form was powered by a 694hp (517kW) Maybach HL 230 P45 petrol engine for a speed of 23mph (37km/h) and a range of 73 miles (117km) with 125 Imp gal (567 litres) of fuel. The vehicle had minimum and maximum armour thicknesses of 26 and 110mm (1.02 and 4.33in) respectively, and the armour was of welded steel with mortised joints. The primary armament was one 3.465in (88mm) L/56 gun with a total of 92 rounds of ammunition, and the secondary armament comprised two or three 0.312in (7.82mm) machine-guns with a total of 5,100 rounds of ammunition: these guns were disposed as one co-axial weapon, one weapon in the bow plate, and one optional weapon in the anti-aircraft position on top of the turret.

introduced on the Ausf E was used in this and all later variants. Early examples of the PzKpfw III Ausf H retained the 50mm KWK L/42 gun, but later examples were produced with the more capable kWK 39 L/60 weapon of the same calibre and this was retrofitted to tanks already in service.

By the beginning of the campaign against the USSR in June 1941, some 1,500 PzKpfw III tanks were in service, and these performed creditably in the opening stages of the campaign. The experience of the crews and the relative maturity of the basic design swept Soviet armour away without difficulty. But from the end of 1941, the new breed of Soviet tanks, epitomized by the T-34 medium and KV heavy types, began to appear in growing numbers: the Soviet tank crews were of better tactical quality, but more importantly, the protection of their vehicles proved too thick for effective penetration by the L/42 gun. A crash programme was launched to retrofit the German tanks with the L/60 gun. To the dismay of the German authorities this longer version of the 50mm gun also proved inadequate to the task of tackling the T-34 and KV, except at point-blank ranges that were seldom achievable on the Eastern Front. A longer-term implication was that Hitler, on learning that his earlier instructions to fit the L/60 weapon had not been obeyed immediately, began to take a more personal interest in the design and manufacture of German tanks, as well as in their deployment and tactical use.

The comparatively small diameter of the PzKpfw III's turret ring now proved the decisive factor in developing a more capable variant: the 50mm Krupp gun was not entirely satisfactory, but the turret ring diameter effectively prohibited the installation of a high-velocity gun of greater calibre. All the Germans could do, therefore, was to step up production of better-protected models in the forlorn hope that numbers would provide the Panzer arm with an edge over the Soviet tank force. The next production variant was thus the PzKpfw III Ausf J, which was similar to the Ausf H apart from a reduction in hull and turret vision slots to ease manufacture, and an increase in armour protection, resulting in an increased weight of 22.30 tonnes and a slight but significant deterioration in cross-country performance and agility.

The Panzerjäger 38(t), otherwise known as the Marder III, was a specialised anti-tank weapon with a 2.95in (75mm) high-velocity gun located in a fixed barbette mounted above the hull rear of the obsolescent PzKpfw 38(t), which was the German designation for the CKD/Praga TNHP or LT-38 light tank.

The next variant was the Ausf L, which entered production in 1942, the year in which PzKpfw III production attained 2,600 machines. The Ausf L was similar to the late-production Ausf J (with the L/60 main gun) in every external respect but armour, which now included a spaced layer above the superstructure and mantlet. This further increased the nose heaviness already evident in the Ausf J and earlier models retrofitted with the L/60 gun.

In 1942 the PzKpfw III Ausf M also appeared, this being a variant of the Ausf L optimized for mass production by the elimination of the hull vision ports and escape doors. Although the elimination of the hull escape doors might be considered a retrograde step, it should be remembered that these were generally inoperable when essential skirt armour was fitted.

Production of the Ausf M continued into the beginning of 1943, but in 1942 the first examples of the ultimate PzKpfw III variant had appeared. This was the Ausf N, identical to the Ausf M in all respects but armament. In July 1942, Hitler had ordered that the Ausf L should be fitted with the obsolescent 75mm (2.95in)kWK L/24 gun in place of its current 50mm weapon. The German leader's intention was to provide a support tank for heavier tanks such as the PzKpfw VI Tiger, and the designated weapon was the ordnance of early models of the PzKpfw IV. But whereas the 50mm weapon was limited to HE and armour-piercing ammunition, the 75mm (2.95in) weapon could fire armour-piercing, HEAT, HE, Smoke and Case projectiles. The same ordnance was used in the Ausf N, which had revised ammunition stowage. Production amounted to 660 Ausf N tanks in the period from July 1942 to August 1943, the 213 vehicles built in 1943 being modified in production with definitive Schürzen (aprons), comprising 8mm (0.315in) skirts over the running gear and 5mm (0.2in) panels around the turret. Further protection was afforded by Zimmerit paste, of which a 100kg

A similar process was used to create the Panzerjäger IV Nashorn, which was the hull of the PzKpfw IV medium tank used as the basis for a 3.465in (88mm) anti-tank gun on a limited-traverse mounting in the rear-mounted barbette.

(220lb) coating provided protection against magnetically attached mines.

Total production of the PzKpfw III was 5,644, and the type's importance on the development of armoured warfare cannot be exaggerated as it was the primary weapon of the Panzer divisions in their heady days of triumph between 1939 and 1941.

The PzKpfw III's partner through the first half of the war was the PzKpfw IV, whose development up to the Ausf E has been covered in the previous chapter. The first definitive variant of the PzKpfw IV was the PzKpfw Ausf F. Although modelled on the preceding Ausf E, this variant was planned with thicker armour and a longer-barreled 75mm (2.95in) main gun. The armour was to a 50mm (1.97in) rather than 30mm (1.18in) basis, but the longer ordnance was not available in time and the standard kWK L/24 gun had to be fitted. The variant, weighing 22.30 tonnes, was built throughout 1941. When the far superior kWK 40 L/43 gun became available, it was introduced on an Ausf F variant known as the PzKpfw IV Ausf F2, earlier models being retrospectively redesignated PzKpfw IV Ausf F1. The Ausf F2 weighed 23.60 tonnes, and its advent marked an apex in German tank capability.

The Ausf F2 was succeeded by the Ausf G, which was basically similar to its predecessor apart from detail modifications and improved armour, the latter including a thicker top to the superstructure. Field additions often included spaced frontal armour and Schürzen of the types used in the PzKpfw III's later variants for protection against hollow-charge warheads. The L/48 version of the kWK 40 gun was introduced on the Ausf H version of this increasingly important tank. The Ausf H began to leave the production lines in March 1943, and was similar to the Ausf F2 and Ausf G, apart from its use of the longer gun, a revised turret hatch cover, cast rather than fabricated drive sprockets, improved frontal armour of the spaced type, and as a measure of protection for the increasingly vulnerable flanks, 8mm (0.315in) turret and 5mm (0.2in) skirt armour. This resulted in an increase in combat weight to 25.00 tonnes, but the retention of the same 300hp (224kW) engine inevitably caused a loss of performance and agility.

The Panzerjäger concept, in which a large-calibre anti-tank gun was mounted on a limited-traverse mounting in an open-topped barbette built up on the rear hull of an obsolescent tank, proved moderately successful at first, but increasing losses to heavier-armed tanks, artillery fire and aircraft attack later led to the demand for more fully optimised Jagdpanzer types with a lower silhouette, thicker armour and overhead protection. An excellent example of this type is the Jagdpanzer IV, which was the chassis and lower hull of the PzKpfw IV tank with a new upper hull of well-sloped and comparatively thick armour carrying a 2.95in (75mm) high-velocity anti-tank gun.

The PzKpfw VI Tiger, sometimes called the Tiger I to differentiate it from the later and far superior Tiger II or Königstiger, was a very formidable battle tank whose potent gun, thick armour but indifferent performance and agility made it better suited to ambush rather than truly mobile armoured warfare.

By the beginning of 1943, the limitations of the PzKpfw III and IV were clear to field commanders and procurement authorities alike, and in February it was proposed that the PzKpfw IV be entirely supplanted in production by the new PzKpfw V Panther and PzKpfw VI Tiger tanks. In essence the notion was correct, but as men such as General Heinz Guderian were swift to point out, production rates of the newer vehicles were so low that the PzKpfw IV should be retained to maintain the numerical strength of the Panzer arm in the decisive year of 1943, which in the event saw the strategic initiative swing firmly to the Allied nations. Hitler therefore decided that production of the PzKpfw IV should continue at least to the beginning of 1944, and this paved the way for the evolution of the final production variant, the PzKpfw IV Ausf J that began to reach combat units in March 1944.

The designers had taken the lessons of combat firmly to heart and created a variant that was easier to produce and more effective in combat, with higher performance and greater cross-country agility. The Ausf J had thicker frontal armour combined with flank protection by wire mesh screens in place of the heavy skirts of the Ausf F, G and H variants. Earlier models had been provided with a power system plus manual back-up for turret traverse, but in the Ausf J the power traverse system was removed (and the manual system supplanted by a two-speed geared unit) to provide greater fuel capacity. The Ausf J was thus a more capable machine than the Ausf H, and remained in production right to the end of World War II, the total for the two models reaching almost 6,000 chassis (from a total of 9,000 PzKpfw IV tanks) in the last two years of the war.

The PzKpfw IV fought on every German front in World War II, and proved itself one of the most important tanks ever produced. Although it was always armed with a 75mm (2.95in) main gun, the adoption of longer-

barreled ordnances of this calibre allowed the designers to keep the tank up to date with most Western and many Soviet tanks, and when properly handled the PzKpfw IV was a capable adversary.

Up to 1940 the German army was highly satisfied with the versatility of the PzKpfw IV, and was content to opt for the exploitation its development potential rather than the creation of a wholly new type. The army had little reason to doubt the wisdom of its decision until the autumn of 1941, when the German forces driving towards Moscow began to encounter small but increasing numbers of the new Soviet T-34 tank, which immediately displayed itself superior to the PzKpfw IV in all aspects of firepower, protection and mobility. And it was clear to the German army that this was a new tank already mature in its mechanical aspects yet full of development potential in terms of firepower and protection.

The designation Sturmgeschütz III was used for obsolescent PzKpfw III battle tanks converted to the assault gun role with a short-barrel 2.95in (75mm) gun in a low barbette replacing the revolving turret of the baseline tank.

This is a PzKpfw IV medium tank of the World War II period.

In November 1941 a German investigation team assessed a captured T-34 and came to the conclusion that the Soviet tank had significant advantages over German tanks in its sloped armour, large road wheels and long gun. The sloping of the armour offered an effective increase in thickness without the weight penalty of vertical protection of this actual thickness; the large road wheels offered a superior ride, especially across country; and the long gun, hitherto rejected by the Germans as impractical for a number of reasons, offered very high muzzle velocity and therefore a devastating armour-penetrating capability. The inevitable conclusion was that all current German tanks were obsolete in the technical sense, and an immediate programme was launched to produce a counter to the T-34: within days the German armaments ministry contracted with Daimler-Benz and MAN for VK3002 designs to meet a specification that demanded a 30/35 tonne battle tank with a 75mm (2.95in) main gun, well sloped armour to a maximum thickness of 40mm (1.57in) on the sides and 60mm (2.36in) on the front, and a maximum speed of 55km/h (34.1mph). In January 1942 the specification was revised, to include a 60km/h (37.3mph) maximum speed and frontal armour of 60mm (2.36in) on the hull and 100mm (3.94in) on the turret.

The VK3002(DB) and VK3002(MAN) designs were completed in April 1942. The VK3002(DB) was essentially a copy of the T-34, with the turret

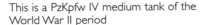

This is a PzKpfw IV medium tank of the World War II period

located so far forward that the driver sat inside the turret cage and had to use a hydraulically operated remote steering system. The VK3002(DB) was a design of great potential, with a diesel engine offering lower susceptibility to fire as well as longer range, but an initial order for 200 vehicles, placed at the instigation of Hitler, was cancelled later in 1942.

The armament ministry, on the other hand, preferred the VK3002(MAN), which was specifically a German solution to the requirement, was powered by a proved petrol engine and, in the short term at least, was better suited to German production practices. The VK3002(MAN) had a basic layout similar to that of the PzKpfw IV, but was considerably more powerful than earlier German tanks, having more than twice the horsepower of the PzKpfW IV, and a special gearbox was developed to allow optimum use of this potential. The rubber-tyred road wheels were of sufficiently great diameter to negate the need for track-return rollers. The turret was located as far back as possible to reduce the type of mobility and tactical problems that might otherwise have been caused by a long barrel overhang of the L/60 gun originally planned for the vehicle (but later replaced by an L/70 weapon).

The first prototype of the VK3002(MAN) appeared in September 1942. It was launched on a large-scale evaluation programme, and such was the seriousness of Germany's armour position on the Eastern Front (compounded by technical problems with the new PzKpfw VI Tiger heavy tank) that the type was ordered into immediate production as the PzKpfw V Panther. The first production Panther appeared in November 1942, and the ambitious production rate of 250 vehicles per month was quickly raised to 600 per month. This figure was never achieved, despite the launch of a large-scale co-production system involving four major

This cutaway view illustrates the major features of the early pattern of Sturmgeschütz III assault gun with an armoured barbette carrying the 2.95in (75mm) short-barrel L/24 gun without a muzzle brake. The lower hull, chassis and tracks were essentially unaltered from those of the PzKpfw III tank on which the vehicle was based.

The PzKpfw VI Tiger was a potent tank killer in confined country, but when caught in the open could be out manoeuvred by larger numbers of Allied tanks and destroyed with shots to the tracks or to the rear of the hull. This is a Tiger destroyed during the closing stages of the fighting in the North African campaign.

manufacturers, and the 1944 monthly average was 330, leading to an overall total of 5,590 Panthers by the end of World War II, comprising 1,850 in the first year of production and 3,740 between January 1944 and May 1945. An additional 679 chassis were completed for use in roles such as recovery, command, artillery observation and tank destroying.

The desired maximum weight limit of 35 tonnes had proved impossible to meet, and the Panther turned the scales at 45.50 tonnes on its service debut. This weight was due mainly to Hitler's insistence on thicker armour, and plans were made for use of the bored-out HL 230 in place of the originally specified HL 210 engine; despite this, the reduced maximum speed of 45km/h (28mph) had to be accepted.

The first 20 Panthers were designated PzKpfw V Panther Ausf A, and were in reality pre-production machines with the thinner frontal armour as demanded by the original specification, a 642hp (479kW) HL 210 engine, an early model of the L/70 main gun and the commander's cupola at the extreme left of the Rheinmetall turret. Considerable development work was undertaken with these first Panthers, which were redesignated PzKpfw V Panther Ausf D1 early in 1943. The proposed second and third production models were the Ausf B with a Maybach Olvar gearbox, and the Ausf C of which no details have been found. Trials with the Ausf A revealed a number of problems, but the importance of the programme was such that no delay in production was authorized to rectify any deficiencies before they were built into service tanks.

The first real production variant was therefore the PzKpfw V Panther Ausf D, which was redesignated PzKpfw V Panther Ausf D2 at the same time that the Ausf A became the Ausf D1. The type appeared in January 1943, and featured the standard type of 'dustbin' cupola, a vision port and machine-gun port in the glacis plate, the definitive L/70 main gun with a double-baffle muzzle brake to reduce recoil distance in an already cramped turret, smoke-dischargers on each side of the turret and, on later production examples, skirt armour added during construction, together with a coating of Zimmerit anti-mine paste.

The next variant appeared in July 1943, and should have been the Ausf E, but for reasons which remain unexplained was in fact designated the

PzKpfw V Panther Ausf A. This incorporated features that had been omitted in order to increase production of the Ausf D2 in preparation for the Germans' final effort to regain the strategic initiative on the Eastern Front in the Battle of Kursk of July 1943, the world's most comprehensive tank battle to date. Kursk was the Panther's combat debut, most available vehicles serving with one army and three SS divisions of the 4th Panzerarmee; when they ran well, the Panthers were more than a match for the Soviets' T-34s, but they seldom travelled for more than a few miles without a mechanical problem, due to the type having been rushed into service prematurely.

The Ausf A introduced the definitive commander's cupola with better ballistic shaping and armoured periscopes, a fully-engineered ball mounting for the hull machine-gun, a monocular rather than binocular gunner's sight in the turret, and elimination of all turret pistol spent-case ejection ports.

The final production variant of the original Panther series was the PzKpfw Panther Ausf G, so designated because Hitler, on 27 February 1944, had ordered the roman numeral in the original designation to be omitted. The origins of this model lay with the February 1942 instruction of the German armaments ministry that MAN was to co-operate with Henschel in the development of a Panther variant, incorporating as many PzKpfw VI Tiger components as possible. The programme would have resulted in the Panther II Ausf F with the interleaved steel wheels of the Tiger II, thicker armour on the hull top, a turret modelled on that of the Tiger Ausf B with stereoscopic rangefinder and gun stabilization system, a higher-rated gearbox, and greater power in the form of the HL 230 rated to 800hp (596kW) with petrol injection and a higher compression ratio, and to 900hp (671kW) with a supercharger.

Known to the Allies as the Royal Tiger or King Tiger, the PzKpfw VI Tiger II or Königstiger was one of the most formidable tanks of World War II, but appeared in only comparatively small numbers from late 1944. The Tiger II carried a longer (L/71 rather than L/56) version of the same 3.465in (88mm) main gun as the Tiger for considerably enhanced offensive power, and was an altogether more capable fighting machine as it had sloped and therefore ballistically more effective armour than its predecessor.

It is hard to overestimate the importance of the Panther to armoured warfare in World War II or to the development of the tank since that time. An indication of the Panther's capabilities is exemplified by its frontal armour, which was impenetrable to the projectiles of the Allies' main gun tanks, while its own manoeuvrability and gun power allowed it to knock out the Allied tanks from stand-off range.

The largest German tanks to see combat in World War II were the variants of the PzKpfw VI Tiger series, which first appeared before the PzKpfw V Panther but which are treated after it because of their later numerical designation. In the late 1930s the German army had started to plan a heavy breakthrough tank, but in 1940 several early schemes were

Although an extremely effective weapon in the type of defensive fighting forced on the Germans in the last campaigns of World War II, the PzKpfw VI Tiger II suffered to an even greater extent than the Tiger from a poor power-to-weight ratio, which adversely affected performance and agility, and at the same time placed so great a strain on the engine and transmission that reliability was worse than that of the Tiger.

PzKpfw VI Ausf B Tiger II

DELIVERED to the extent of just 484 tanks between November 1944 and May 1945, the Tiger II made an enormous impression on the Allies, whose tanks were decidedly outclassed by this German vehicle in terms of firepower and protection. The Tiger II was a heavy tank with a five-man crew, and weighed 69.75 tonnes in combat condition with a full fuel and armament load. The vehicle had an overall length of 34ft 2.5in (10.43m) with the main gun trained directly ahead, its width was 12ft 2.5in (3.72m) and its height was 10ft 9in (3.27m). Power was provided by a 600hp (447kW) Maybach HL 230 P30 petrol engine for a speed of 24mph (38km/h) under ideal conditions, and a range of 68 miles (110km) was possible with the maximum 190 Imp gal (865 litres) of fuel. The Tiger II's minimum and maximum armour thicknesses were 40 and 185mm (1.57 and 7.28in) respectively, and the tank's armament included as its primary element a 3.465in (88mm) gun with 84 rounds of ammunition and as its secondary element two 0.312in (7.92mm) machine-guns (one mounted co-axially with the main gun and the other in the bow plate) with 4,800 rounds of ammunition.

discontinued in favour of a more advanced 30 tonne breakthrough tank armed with a 75mm (2.95in) main gun. Henschel and Porsche each received an order for four VK3001(H) and VK3001(P) prototypes respectively.

The Germans had been working concurrently on a heavier tank concept primarily to satisfy the demands of Hitler, who was becoming a firm advocate of heavy tanks with powerful armament and protection. Hitler's first choice for the main gun was a tank development of the 88mm (3.46in) FlaK 36 dual-role anti-aircraft/anti-tank gun, and armour was to provide protection against a similar gun. Competing VK4501(H) and VK4501(P) prototypes were introduced in May 1941. The contracts stipulated that the prototypes should be ready for Hitler's birthday on 20 April 1942: each type was to use a Krupp-designed turret accommodating the 88mm (3.46in) kWK 36 L/56 gun. The VK3601(H) was proposed as the VK3601(H1) with the Krupp turret and an 88mm (3.46in) gun and as the VK3601(H2) with a Rheinmetall turret and a 75mm (2.95in) kWK 42 L/70 gun. The H2 variant was never built, but the first prototypes of the VK3601(H1) variant appeared in March 1942.

The VK4501(P) appeared in the following month, and was modelled on the VK3001(P) with the same type of petrol-electric drive and longitudinal torsion bar suspension. Comparative trials confirmed the overall superiority of the VH4501(H), although it was as much as 11.00 tonnes over legend weight, and in August 1942 the type was ordered into production under the designation PzKpfw VI Tiger Ausf H and with the primary armament of onekWK 36 gun.

Variously known as the Sturmtiger and Sturmmörser Tiger, this extraordinary vehicle was the result of the German army's request for a very well protected 8.27in (210mm) self-propelled howitzer based on the PzKpfw VI Ausf E Tiger for the infantry support role and therefore able to tackle hard targets with high-angle fire. There was no suitable weapon for this vehicle, however, and it was therefore decided to develop a type offering basically similar capabilities by using the 14.96in (380mm) Raketenwerfer 61, which was an army development of a weapon initially developed for the German navy as an anti-submarine mortar. Only 10 such vehicles were completed, the raised superstructure carrying the massive mortar and 12 rounds.

Production of the Tiger lasted exactly two years from August 1942, and during that time amounted to 1,350 vehicles. Production peaked in April 1944, when 104 vehicles were delivered: the original rate planned by the armaments ministry had been 12 vehicles per month, but at Hitler's insistence this figure had been increased to 25 vehicles per month by November 1942, increasing again as the type proved itself in combat. In February 1944 the designation was revised, and the vehicle became the PzKpfw Tiger Ausf E (SdKfz 181), this change being contemporary with a modification of the production standard to include a new cupola, simplified fittings and resilient steel wheels in place of the original type with rubber tyres.

The Tiger was truly a massive machine, and its design epitomizes that of the classic 'German tank' of World War II: this was evolved before the T-34 hammered home the advantages of sloped armour, and the Tiger was thus the next in logical sequence from the PzKpfw IV with basically upright armour. In so large and heavy a machine the designers were faced with acute problems of hull rigidity, especially against the torsional effect of recoil when the gun was fired at any angle off the centreline. For this reason the basic structure made use of the largest possible one-piece plates. The overall impression conveyed by the vehicle was one of angular strength, and was confirmed by the minimal armour inclination and maximum armour thickness for a combat weight of 55.00 tonnes or more. The movement of this mass required considerable power: the first 250 vehicles had the 642hp (479kW) Maybach HL 210 P45 petrol engine, and the remainder had the 694hp (517.5kW) HL 230 P45 from the same manufacturer.

The main tactical limitations of the Tiger were the use of hydraulic power from an engine-driven motor for turret traverse, meaning that the heavy turret had to be moved in secondary manual mode when the engine was shut down, and the prodigious thirst of the engine, which resulted in very short range and the general use of the Tiger as an ambush tank rather than a mobile warfare tank, and the high points of its career were thus in the close-country campaigns such as those waged in Normandy (June and July 1944) and the Ardennes (December 1944).

As the Tiger entered production, the Germans decided to develop a new model with better armament and protection in case the Soviets produced another surprise after the T-34. Henschel and Porsche were asked to develop competing designs with sloped armour and the new kWK 43 88mm (3.46in) gun. This weapon was considerably heavier and longer than the kWK 36, but its L/71 barrel provided a much higher muzzle velocity for enhanced armour-penetrating capability.

Porsche responded with the VK4502(P), based on the VK4501(P) but carrying a beautifully shaped turret offering excellent ballistic protection and initially intended for a 150mm (5.91in) L/37 or 105mm (4.13in) L/70 gun, later revised to an 88mm (3.46in) L/71 gun in line with the army's thinking of the period. The VK4502(P) was considered the likely winner by Porsche, which organized the casting process for the turret before the receipt of any production order: but whereas the petrol-electric drive of the VK4501(P) had been rejected largely for its novelty, the basically similar system of the VK4502(P) was now rejected because the copper required for its electric motors was, by late 1943, in very short supply.

The winning design was therefore Henschel's VK4503(H), although the first 50 production vehicles were fitted with the Porsche turret before the comparable Henschel type became standard. The Porsche turret was recognizable by the cut-away lower edge of the turret front, creating a dangerous shot trap between the gun and the roof of the hull; the Henschel turret had a straight front dropping right down to the hull roof without the Porsche turret's dangerous re-entrant. The Henschel design had been completed later than anticipated, the delay to October 1943 being attributable mainly to the armament ministry's desire to standardize as many parts as possible between the new tank and the planned Panther II. Henschel thereby lost a considerable amount of time in liaison with MAN. Production finally began in December 1943, alongside the Tiger (now sometimes known as the Tiger I to differentiate it from its more powerful companion), and the type entered service in the spring of 1944, first seeing action on the Eastern Front in May 1944. Production continued to the end of World War II, and amounted to 485 vehicles, known to the Allies as the Royal Tiger or King Tiger, to the German soldiers as the Königstiger (King Tiger) and to German officialdom as the PzKpfw VI Tiger II Ausf B, this was revised at about the time of the tank's introduction to PzKpfw Tiger II Ausf B.

To a certain extent, the Tiger II should be regarded as the heavyweight counterpart to the Panther rather than as a successor to the Tiger; certainly, the Tiger II had similarities to the Panther in its configuration, sloped armour, and powerplant. This comprised a 694hp (517kW) Maybach HL 230 P30 petrol engine for a 69.70 tonne vehicle, considerably heavier than the 45.50 tonne Panther and the 55.00 tonne Tiger I. The results were inevitable: reduced performance and agility as the power-to-weight ratio was poorer than that of the Panther and Tiger, unreliability because the engine and transmission were overstressed, and a dismal maximum range. These failings were perhaps excusable in a tank now used for defensive warfare, its sole offensive outing being the 'Battle of the Bulge' of December 1944, when many Tiger IIs broke down or ran out of fuel.

On the credit side, however, the Tiger II was the heaviest, the best-armed and best-protected tank of World War II. The construction of the vehicle was of welded and well-sloped armour varying in thickness from 25mm (0.98in) on the belly to a maximum of 150mm (5.91in) on the hull upper front; the turret was also welded of armour up to 100mm (3.94in) thick.

Germany's massive tanks of the Panther and Tiger series were good vehicles, using their firepower and protection to counter the Allies' numerical superiority in armoured vehicles of all types, but were finally immobilized for want of petrol. The significance of these operational tanks is proved by the interest with which captured examples were examined by the victorious Western Allies, their many good features being assessed for incorporation into the new generation of American and British post-war tanks.

Germany's primary allies in World War II were Italy and Japan, but these fell far behind Germany in the development and employment of armour as the cornerstone of their land operations. It has to be admitted that both countries lacked an industrial base comparable in size with that of Germany, but this merely compounded the problem that neither country had seriously considered the tank as an offensive weapon in its own right, and therefore laid the organizational and tactical groundwork for significant armoured forces in the early to mid-1930s.

The best Italian tank of the period was the 14.50 tonne Carro Armato M.14/41 of which 1,103 examples were built with the 145hp (108kW) SPA 15 TM41 engine, sand-removing air filters, and a primary armament of one 47mm gun. The final development in this design sequence was the 15.50 tonne Carro Armato M.15/42, which entered service in 1943. This was modelled closely on the M.14/41, but had a hull lengthened to permit the installation of a 192hp (143kW) SPA 15 TBM42 petrol engine. Several detail modifications (such as additional attachment points for external stowage,

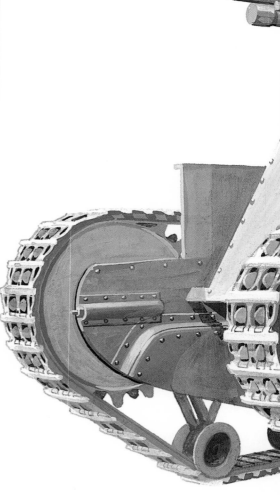

The Japanese fighting vehicle known as the Medium Tank Type 89 was powered by a diesel engine for reduced vulnerability and for the better fuel economy typical of this type of powerplant, but was otherwise of undistinguished design with riveted armour and a forward-mounted turret carrying the main armament, which was a 57mm gun that was complemented by two machine-guns.

and a revised exhaust system) were introduced and the turret was provided with a power traverse system. The armament was also modernized, the 47/32 gun of the M.13/40 and M.14/41 being replaced in the M 15/42 by a 47/40 gun whose additional eight calibres of barrel length provided a higher muzzle velocity for greater armour penetration without any sacrifice of fire rate, which remained about seven or eight rounds per minute. Production of the M.15/42 totalled about 90 examples by March 1943, after which time the Italians decided to halt manufacture.

The best Japanese tank of the World War II period was the Medium Tank Type 3 (Chi-Nu). This was based on the hull of the Chi-He with a new turret designed around the Type 3 gun and installed on the basic hull. The larger main gun and its turret (without a machine-gun in its rear face) increased combat weight to 18.80 tonnes, but as the 240hp (179kW) diesel engine remained unchanged, the overall effect was a slight reduction in performance. Production started in 1944, but Japan's increasingly acute production problems limited manufacture to between 50 and 60 of these improved tanks.

Given their failure to appreciate the true course of development in armoured warfare in the 1930s, the Italian and Japanese tank arms could not emulate that of Germany either operationally or technically. Italian and Japanese tanks were therefore only of limited use in World War II, and generally failed to inspire post-war trends.

The Allies Fight Back

AT the outbreak of World War II in September 1939, British armoured regiments were equipped with tanks developed in the 1930s, but the increasingly rapid pace of re-armament since 1936 was beginning to pay dividends in newer tank types, which the army hoped would be better suited to the type of operations likely to be encountered in Britain's worldwide commitments. These commitments required tanks that could operate in terrains, climates and logistical situations as diverse as northern Europe, North Africa and the Middle/Near East, and South-East Asia.

The tank types serving in greatest numbers at the beginning of World War II were the Light Tank Mk VI, the Infantry Tanks Mk I and Mk II, and the Cruiser Tanks Mk I, Mk II, Mk III and Mk IV. The best of these, without doubt, were the A13 Cruiser Tank Mk III and A13 Mk II Cruiser Tank Mk IV, and the A12 Infantry Tank Mk II Matilda II, all of which werel discussed in the second chapter.

In the cruiser category, great things had been expected of the A13 Mk III Cruiser Tank Mk V Covenanter, but this machine had not performed well and in 1937 the basic design was developed into the A15 Cruiser Tank Mk VI Crusader, first of the so-called heavy cruiser tanks but with the same 2pdr (40mm) main armament as the earlier tanks together with the 340hp (253.5kW) Liberty Mk III engine used in the A13. Even as it appeared, the type was recognized as being too lightly armed and too poorly armoured. The Crusader was nonetheless ordered 'off the drawing board' in July 1939, nine companies being involved in manufacture of an eventual 5,300 examples in various marks.

The hull was similar to that of the Covenanter, with a long low decking and a well-angled glacis, and the Christie type of running gear was also similar to that of the Covenanter, although with the addition of an extra road wheel on each side and with the springs located inside rather than outside the hull. The running gear proved to be excellent, and the Crusader was able to exceed its legend speed of 27mph (43.5km/h) by a considerable margin: some Crusaders were capable of speeds over 40mph (64.4km/h), but high speeds often caused mechanical failure in the engine. The forward compartment was occupied by the driver and bow machine-gunner, the latter operating a single 7.92mm (0.31in) Besa machine-gun in a small turret to the left of the driver. The rear compartment was occupied by the Liberty engine, a de-rated version of the aero engine designed in World War II as a 400hp (298kW) unit. The centre of the vehicle housed the fighting compartment with the multi-side and angular (though well sloped) turret above it: this power-traversed turret was extremely cramped with its complement of commander, gunner and loader/radio operator, and carried only a 2pdr (40mm) main gun, whose limitations were becoming apparent

This cutaway illustration highlights the most important structural and conceptual features of the classic Sherman medium tank in its M4A4 variant that was standardized in February 1942 and powered by a 30-cylinder Chrysler petrol engine that comprised five six-cylinder car engines geared together to operate as a single unit offering 425hp (317kW) for a speed of 25mph (40km/h). The M4A4 had a crew of five and a combat weight of 31.7 tons, and its armament comprised one 2.95in (75mm) main gun and three machine-guns.

even in 1939. A 7.92mm (0.31in) Besa machine-gun was mounted co-axially with the main armament, and there was also a 0.303in (7.7mm) Bren light machine-gun on the roof for anti-aircraft defence. In the Cruiser Tank Mk VICS Crusader ICS the 2pdr (40mm) gun was replaced by a 3 in (76.2mm) howitzer for use in the close-support role.

The Crusader was rushed into production and service before all its mechanical problems had been eliminated, and in its first combat operations, the 'Battleaxe' fighting of June 1941, more Crusaders were immobilized by mechanical failure than by enemy action. There was also criticism of the Crusader's cramped interior and thin armour, resulting in the Cruiser Tank Mk VIA Crusader II. The first criticism was alleviated by omission of the machine-gun turret, although the space was frequently used to increase the 2pdr (40mm) ammunition stowage; the second was ameliorated by increasing the maximum armour thickness on the frontal arc to 49mm (1.93in). The loss of the turret was balanced by the thicker armour, and the combat weight therefore remained steady at 19.30 tonnes. There was also a Cruiser Tank Mk VIA Crusader IICS with a 3in (76.2mm) close-support howitzer replacing the 2pdr (40mm) gun.

The ultimate development of the Crusader gun tank was the 20.07 tonne Cruiser Tank Crusader III, with much improved armament and the improved Liberty Mk IV engine. In this model all provision for the machine-gun turret was removed, the frontal armour was thickened and the main gun became a 6pdr (57mm) weapon. This gun was both longer and heavier than its predecessor, and this led to revision of the turret for two-man operation by the gunner and commander/loader/radio operator. The Crusader III was

available in time for the decisive 2nd Battle of El Alamein in October and November 1942, but was severely hampered operationally by the overtaxing of the commander. Nevertheless, the Crusader was a vital element of the eventual British success in the North African campaign, and although a few were used in the opening stages of the Italian campaign, the Crusader disappeared rapidly as a first-line gun tank from mid-1943.

The origins of the cruiser concept lay with the lightweight cavalry tank, designed for reconnaissance and deep penetration, using its speed and mobility to avoid the type of trouble that could be handled by thin armour and light armament. The Crusader was the last cruiser tank to be designed to this concept, whose fallacies were evidenced by the efforts made to step up the Crusader's protection and firepower.

The 6pdr (57mm) gun offered the firepower required, so the main problem to be addressed in the next cruiser tank was the deficiency in protection. Early in 1941, the War Office issued a requirement for a new heavy cruiser tank, to be called the Cromwell.

This requirement demanded armour on a 2.75in (70mm) basis, thereby offering some 50 per cent more protection than available on the Crusader, and a 6pdr (57mm) main armament in a turret using a 60in (1.52m) diameter turret ring so that there would be adequate space for the commander, gunner and loader. The requirement also specified a combat weight of about 25.2 tonnes for the new tank, which was to be powered by a Rolls-Royce Meteor (a derivative of the Merlin aero engine) to provide cruiser-type performance. Progress was hindered because the Meteor engine was still at an early stage of development by Leyland and Rolls-Royce.

Known to its American originators as the Light Tank M3 and to the British as the General Stuart, this attractive little vehicle was universally known as the 'Honey' for its pleasant nature and great reliability. Carrying a four-man crew and weighing some 12.3 tons, the M3 was powered by a 250hp (186kW) Continental radial engine for a speed of 35mph (56km/h), was armed with a 37mm main gun equipped with a primitive stabilisation system, and also had between three and five machine-guns.

Development of the A27M Cruiser Tank Mk VIII Cromwell was also delayed by the exhaustive evaluation programme demanded by the War Office following the problems with the production runs of the Liberty-engined interim Crusader and Cavalier models. Although the first Cromwell prototype had run in January 1942, it was January 1943 before the first Cromwell I gun tanks came off the production line. The first vehicles had the 600hp (447kW) Meteor engine built by Rolls-Royce, although production of this important engine was switched as rapidly as possible to other manufacturers so that Rolls-Royce could concentrate on its aero engine development and production programmes. The availability of the new engine finally gave British tanks the performance fillip they needed: there was now great reliability and ample power, and the engine rarely needed to be run at the high power settings that had caused the less powerful Liberty to break down with such regularity.

The Cromwell had been planned with the 6pdr (57mm) gun, but during 1942 there was a gradual change in popularity from the dedicated anti-tank gun to a weapon capable of firing anti-tank and HE rounds. Officers with experience of the American M3 Grant and M4 Sherman tanks were unanimous in their praise for the 75mm (2.95in) M2 and M3 weapons used in these vehicles, and their pressure finally convinced the War Office. In January 1943 it was decided that the majority of medium tanks should be fitted with a dual-capable weapon, and be supported in action by smaller numbers of tanks with role-specific anti-tank and close-support weapons. The result in the armament field was the rapid procurement of the 75mm (2.95in) Mk 5/5A gun, derived from the 6pdr (57mm) weapon with the barrel bored out, shortened and fitted with a single-baffle muzzle brake and firing the standard range of US ammunition for the M2/M3 guns.

It was planned to fit this weapon in the Cromwell, whose generous turret ring diameter made such a move possible without undue modification, but as the weapon did not become available until October 1943, the first Cromwells were delivered with the 6pdr (57mm) gun. In overall

Seen here with a flail-type mineclearing system extended in front of its nose, the M4A1 was the second production version of the Sherman medium tank, and was powered by a 400hp (298kW) Continental R-975 radial engine for a speed of 24mph (39km/h) at a weight of 29.7 tons and with a crew of five. The armament was of the standard type for these early variants, namely one 2.95in (75mm) main gun and three machine-guns.

configuration the Cromwell was of typical British tank layout, with Christie-type running gear derived from that of the A13 with suitable strengthening.

The Cromwell remained in service until 1950, and went through an extensive development programme, involving the introduction of the Cromwell I with an armament of one 6pdr (57mm) gun and two 7.92mm (0.31in) Besa machine-guns; the Cromwell II with tracks 15.5in (394mm) rather than 14in (356mm) wide to reduce ground pressure and promote agility; the Cromwell III (originally designated Cromwell X) produced by converting the Centaur I with the Meteor engine; the Cromwell IV conversion of the Centaur III with the Meteor engine and a 75mm (2.95in) gun; the Cromwell V improvement of the basic tank with the 75mm gun; the Cromwell Vw with a welded rather than riveted hull; the Cromwell VI close-support version fitted with a 3.7in (94mm) howitzer in place of the 75mm (2.95in) gun; the Cromwell VII based on the Mk IV but fitted with wider tracks, a reduced ratio final drive and increased armour thickness for a combat weight of 28.45 tonnes; the Cromwell VIIw with a welded hull; and the final-production Cromwell VIII development of the Cromwell VI close-support version with the improvements of the Cromwell VII.

The Cromwell proved itself an excellent tank in terms of protection and mobility, and when properly handled could evade the more powerfully armed German tanks. But this could not disguise the fact, recognized at the beginning of 1942, that the type would soon lack the firepower necessary to combat new German tanks likely to appear in service from late 1942. This

The A27M, otherwise known as the Cruiser Tank Mk VIII Cromwell, was the full-development version of the A27L or Cruiser Tank Mk VIII Centaur with the earlier tank's 395hp (294.5kW) Liberty engine replaced by the considerably more powerful 600hp (447kW) Rolls-Royce Meteor engine for a maximum speed of 40mph (64km/h) at a weight of 28 tons. The Cromwell had a crew of five, and its main armament was one 2.95in (75mm) gun.

resulted in a development known as the A30 Cruiser Tank Challenger, designed to carry the very powerful 17pdr (3in/76.2mm) anti-tank gun in a new and enlarged turret. This turret was characterized by its height rather than its width, and despite the lengthening of the Cromwell's basic hull by the addition of a sixth road wheel on each side, the 32.00 tonne Challenger was too small for its turret and performance suffered as a consequence. The pressures of the situation demanded production, however, and in 1943 some 260 Challengers were ordered: these were generally used to strengthen the capabilities of Cromwell cruiser tank regiments in the North-West European campaign of 1944-45.

The last operational cruiser tank was another heavy type, the A34 Cruiser Tank Comet. The specific spur for the specification that led to development of the Comet was the nature of the armoured battles fought in the Western Desert early in 1942, when it became clear that current British tanks lacked a gun capable of defeating the armour of Germany's latest tanks. Just as worrying was the fact that the new generation of British tanks was designed round the 6pdr (57mm) gun, which was only marginally superior to current German protection. The answer was a larger-calibre gun, and the ideal weapon was found in the 17pdr (3in/76.2mm) towed anti-tank gun. Plans to upgrade the Cromwell with this weapon proved impossible, and the hybrid Challenger was also unsuccessful. Just one month after the appearance of the prototype Challenger in August 1942, the decline of the British situation in North Africa further emphasized the need for an up-gunned cruiser tank, and in September, Leyland was commissioned to design a new A34 heavy cruiser tank with the 17pdr gun and good armour on a chassis that was to use as many Cromwell features as possible in order to reduce costs and speed development.

Leyland had completed its A34 mock-up by September 1943 after starting definitive work in July, and production was scheduled for mid-1944. The hull was based on that of the Cromwell (and thereby perpetuated the vertical front plate and bow machine-gun that had caused a certain amount of justified criticism), but the armour was thickened and the construction was all-welded. The same 600hp (447kW) Meteor engine and associated transmission were used, and the running gear was ultimately revised to include four track-return rollers on each side. The major improvement, however, was the welded turret with a cast front plate and mantlet: this turret was more spacious, had better access, supported a 360-degree vision cupola for the commander, was fitted with an electrical traverse system, and had provision for the ready-use rounds to be stowed in armoured bins for additional protection.

The prototype appeared in February 1944 with running gear akin to that of the Cromwell. But the need to strengthen the suspension for the Comet's weight of 33.34 tonnes combined with other modifications to delay production into the late summer, the first production tanks reaching the

Although not a tank in any real sense of the word, the Landing Vehicle Tracked may be regarded in some respects as the analogue of the tank and armoured personnel carrier for the amphibious assault role, and some later types were indeed fitted with the turreted armament of a light tank for the direct support of landed troops. This is an LVT(A) armed with two 20mm cannon.

To the British and US armies the US Navy's LVT(A)4 was known as the Alligator Mk IV, and was a six-man vehicle used mainly in the support role with the power-traversed turret of the M8 Howitzer Motor Carriage with its short 2.95in (75mm) howitzer. The LVT(A)4 weighed 18.3 tons fully laden, and with a 250hp (186kW) Continental radial engine had water and land speeds of 7 and 16mph (11.25 and 25.75km/h) respectively.

regiments in September 1944. Thereafter the Comet proved itself an excellent machine that remained in British service until 1958, and apart from the high-quality main armament, its most notable features were its cross-country speed and agility: these factors were often too great for the crew to endure, and the tank therefore has the distinction of being limited by crew rather than by mechanical considerations.

The British army's first two infantry tanks, the Matilda I and II, had resulted from official requirements and specifications. The same cannot be said for their successor, the Valentine, which was a private venture by Vickers-Armstrongs, based on the A10 Cruiser Tank Mk II with components from a number of other Vickers-Armstrongs tanks of the period, notably the A9 Cruiser Tank Mk I and A11 Infantry Tank Mk I. The resulting vehicle was a hybrid of the pure infantry tank and the cruiser tank: the protection and armament were to infantry tank standards, but the performance fell between infantry and cruiser tank requirements, an unfortunate feature that led the War Office to regard the machine as a well-protected cruiser, allocating it to the new armoured divisions being raised in expectation of the open warfare for which the Valentine really lacked the performance.

The company presented its design to the War Office in February 1938, but it was July 1939 before a production order for the Infantry Tank Mk III Valentine was placed and, given the exigencies of the situation, this order demanded 275 tanks delivered in the shortest possible time. No prototype was required as the basic features of the design had already been well proved, and the first Valentine I entered service in May 1940, coinciding with the German offensive against the West. Production ended in the early months of 1944 after some 8,275 had been built. Of these, almost 2,700 (including all but 30 of the 1,420 Canadian-built machines) were supplied to the USSR. The Red Army approved the Valentine's simplicity, reliability and protection, but found the main armament hopelessly inadequate: the standard 2pdr (40mm) gun of the British tanks was often replaced in Soviet service by a 76.2mm (3in) weapon which boosted offensive performance to a considerable degree, but made the already small turret yet more cramped.

Mention has been made of some of the Valentine's virtues, and to these must be added the type's enormous advantage of easy upgrading in terms of armament and motive power. Up to the Mk VIII model, all Valentines

weighed 16.26 tonnes. The Valentine I was powered by a 135hp (101kW) AEC petrol engine, had a crew of three, and the small turret accommodated commander and the gunner for the 2pdr (40mm) main gun, which was supported by a 7.92mm (0.31in) Besa co-axial machine-gun: the commander also acted as gunner and radio operator, and this proved a serious hindrance to the proper exercise of his basic function. The Valentine II had a 131hp (97.7kW) AEC diesel engine, but was otherwise similar to the Valentine I although often fitted with sand shields for desert operations. The Valentine III was identical with the Valentine II in everything except its turret, which was a modified type allowing a three-man fighting crew: the turret had the appearance of the original turret, but was modified internally by pushing the front plate forward and the rear plate backward. The Valentine IV and V were identical with the Mk II and Mk III respectively except in the engine, which was a 138hp (103kW) General Motors diesel. The Valentine VI and VII were produced in Canada, and were in effect versions of the Valentine IV with a General Motors diesel engine, a cast rather than riveted nose plate, and a 0.3in (7.62mm) Browning rather than a Besa co-axial machine-gun: the Mk VII differed from the Mk VI in having a remote-control system for the machine-gun. The Valentine VIIA was a derivative of the Mk VII with studded tracks and jettisonable external fuel tanks.

Seen with its flotation skirt lowered, this is a Duplex Drive version of the infantry Tank Mk III Valentine XI with all-welded construction and a primary armament of one 2.95in (75mm) gun. Attached in watertight fashion to the hull, the skirt was erected by release of compressed gas into tubes that thus straightened and lifted the canvas screen (skirt) attached to them.

The Valentine VIII received a considerable improvement in firepower by the adoption of a 6pdr (57mm) main gun, although its installation sacrificed the co-axial machine-gun in the two-man turret; the 6pdr (57mm) gun was controlled in elevation via a geared manual system, the original 2pdr (40mm) weapon having been operated directly via a gunner's shoulder rest. Weight was increased to 17.27 tonnes, and power was provided by the AEC diesel, switched in the otherwise identical Valentine IX to the General Motors diesel. Some Mk IXs were later fitted with a 165hp (123kW) General Motors diesel, and this engine was also used in the last two production models, the Valentine X with a 6pdr (57mm) main gun and Besa co-axial machine-gun, and the Valentine XI with a cast nose plate and a 75mm (2.95in) gun in place of the 6pdr (57mm) weapon.

After the Valentine came the United Kingdom's most important infantry tank of World War II, the A22 Infantry Tank Mk IV Churchill. This vehicle was planned in 1939 as a replacement for the Matilda II, the operational scenario envisaged by the War Office comprising a Western Front not dissimilar to that in France during World War I. This scenario called for a tank that was in essence a modern version of the rhomboidal tanks of that war, with thick armour, good but not exceptional armament, and the ability to move without undue difficulty in a heavily shelled area. In September 1939 the specification for an A20 infantry tank was issued, and design work was entrusted to Harland & Wolff in Belfast, as part of the government's policy of diversifying tank design and construction capability. Harland & Wolff built four prototypes by June 1940, and these revealed a striking similarity to World War I practices, with a general rhomboidal shape for good trench-crossing capability, and a main armament of two 2pdr (40mm) guns located in side sponsons. The type was also planned with a central turret, but none of the prototypes was fitted with either turret or armament.

In June 1940 the French campaign ended, and with it the War Office discarded its notions of latter-day trench warfare, and thus the A20's *raison*

The Valentine Crocodile was a development vehicle for the armoured flamethrower concept, and was the basic gun tank revised with the flame gun in a small turret: fuel was supplied by gas pressure from an armoured two-wheel trailer towed behind the truck.

One of the many Valentine variants used for development purposes was this flail type, with a powered drum supported ahead of the vehicle to thrash the ground with the chains and explode any pressure-activated anti-tank mines buried there.

d'être. The design had good features in its hull and running gear, however, and these formed the basis of the tank designed to meet the revised A22 specification released to Vauxhall Motors. The country's desperate situation after the defeat at Dunkirk was reflected in the War Office's stipulation that production of the A22 should begin within one year, even though it realized that so hasty a programme would necessarily entail a number of inbuilt faults in the first model. Design began in July 1940 and the first A22 prototype appeared in December 1940, with the initial Churchill I production tanks appearing in June 1941, to inaugurate a programme that finally produced 5,640 Churchill tanks before production was completed in October 1945.

Results of tank development in the late 1930s, and the lessons of the Polish and Western campaigns waged and won by the Germans in 1939 and 1940, led to a tank that was both lower and better protected than its predecessors. In the first Churchills, the armour varied in thickness from 16mm (0.63in) to 102mm (4in), but two short-term limitations were the inadequate armament and the problem-prone engine. By 1940 it had been realized that the 2pdr (40mm) gun was too feeble a weapon for effective anti-tank employment, and lacked a significant HE shell capability; a considerably more effective weapon, the 6pdr (57mm) gun, was already in existence but not in production, and in the days after Dunkirk, a decision was made to keep the obsolescent gun in large-scale production rather than phase in the 6pdr (57mm) weapon. As far as the Churchill was concerned, this meant that a substantial 39.12 tonne vehicle was fitted with a turret carrying obsolescent armament. The situation was partially remedied in the Churchill I by the installation of a 3in (76.2mm) howitzer in the front plate of the hull: this howitzer had a useful support capability, although the installation was restricted by the limited traverse imposed by the semi-recessed position of the front plate behind the projecting forward horns of the running gear. The crew of five comprised the driver and gunner in the nose compartment, and the commander, gunner and loader in the spacious turret.

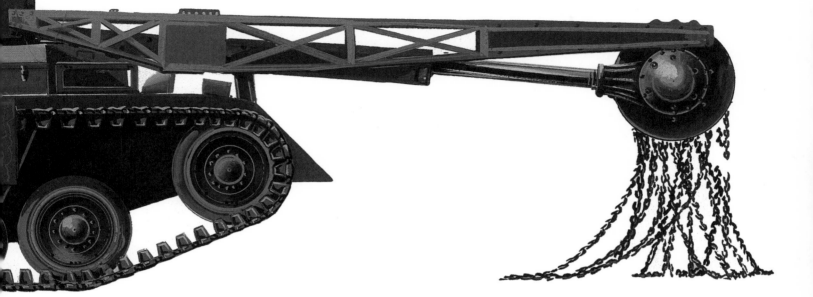

Many of the special-purpose 'funny' variants evolved with Valentine series prototypes were then developed into operational models based on the A22, otherwise known as the Infantry Tank Mk IV Churchill. One of the most important such variants of the Churchill was the AVRE (Armoured Vehicle Royal Engineers), which was a conversion from Churchill III or IV for assault engineer units with the main gun replaced by a petard mortar firing demolition bombs, with special stowage bins for engineer equipment, and with special exterior fittings on the front and sides for role-specific attachments. The vehicle illustrated here is a further development of the AVRE by the Canadian army as the Churchill AVRE Mk II SBG with a 34ft (10.4m) Standard Box Girder bridge that could be laid across a gap and then released.

The other major limitation was the engine, a custom-designed Bedford petrol unit that was essentially a pair of six-cylinder truck engines lying on their sides and married to a common crank-case. This petrol unit developed only 350hp (261kW), giving the Churchill a distinctly modest power-to-weight ratio, and was also plagued with reliability problems in its first year of service. Unreliability was a disadvantage in itself, but it was exacerbated by the Churchill's poor engine installation. The War Office had demanded a readily accessible engine compartment, but this failed to materialize and even comparatively minor problems demanded the removal of the entire engine. Development and service experience gradually eliminated the engine problems, and this in turn reduced the adverse effect of the poor engine installation. Ultimately the Churchill became a notably reliable tank.

The Churchill was in service with the British army from 1941 to 1952, and in this period underwent considerable development, especially during World War II. The Churchill I has already been described in basic detail, and there was also a Churchill I CS with a second 3in (76.2mm) howitzer in the turret in place of the 2pdr (40mm) gun. The Churchill II was similar to the Churchill I in all but armament, where the hull-mounted howitzer was replaced by a 7.92mm (0.31in) Besa machine-gun to complement the co-axial weapon in the turret. These first two marks may be regarded as pilot models, and the A22 design began to reach maturity in the Churchill III, which was a much improved 39.63 tonne model that appeared in March 1942 with an all-welded turret accommodating the 6pdr (57mm) gun for greater anti-tank capability; the Mk III also introduced the large mudguards that were fitted on all later marks and retrofitted to the first two variants. The Churchill IV was similar to the Mk III except for its turret, which was cast rather than welded; in North Africa, some Mk IVs were revised to the so-called Churchill IV (NA 75) standard with the 75mm (2.95in) main gun and 0.3in (7.62mm) Browning co-axial

Another use for the Churchill AVRE was the creation of paths across dry gaps by the dropping of a large fascine.

machine-gun of the M3 Grant medium tank. The Churchill V was the first genuine close-support version of the series, and was armed with a 3.7in (94mm) Tank Howitzer Mk 1, the same weapon as that installed in the Centaur IV. The final variant of the initial Churchill series was the Churchill VI, another gun tank, and modelled on the Mk IV with the exception of the main armament, which was a 75mm (2.95in) Mk 5 weapon of the type installed on the Centaur III and on the Cromwell V, VI and VII.

The Churchill VI was essentially an interim variant pending deliveries of the considerably upgraded A22F (later A42) Infantry Tank Churchill VII. The origins of the variant date back to the War Office's realization that appliqué armour was not the optimum solution to the problem of improving protection. The A22F specification therefore called for a maximum armour thickness of 152mm (6in), but this was to be of the integral rather than appliqué type. The resultant Churchill VII retained the basic configuration and shape of the earlier marks, but was extensively revised to allow the incorporation of thicker armour in the structure and the addition of many features shown to be desirable in earlier variants. The armour varied in thickness from 25mm (0.98in) to 152mm (6in), and this increased the tank's basic weight to 40.64 tonnes. The engine remained unaltered so the performance was degraded, and the main armament was the same 75mm (2.95in) gun as fitted in the Mk VI, with a single-baffle muzzle brake; the turret was a composite unit with the horizontal roof welded to the cast vertical sections, and was the first

British example of a commander's cupola providing a 360-degree field of vision in the closed-down mode.

The close-support version of the Mk VII was the Churchill VIII, the last production variant. This was identical to the Mk VII in all but its armament, which was the same as that of the Mk V: one 3.7in (94mm) howitzer and two 7.92mm (0.31in) Besa machine-guns, one co-axial and the other in the bow plate.

The last three marks were earlier Churchills reworked to improved standards, with appliqué armour and the cast turret of the Mk VII complete with the 75mm (2.95in) gun. The designations Churchill IX, X and XI were used for Mks III and IV, Mk VI and Mk V tanks respectively, while the suffix LT (Light turret) was used for those that retained their original turrets (revised for the heavier main gun) but featured appliqué armour.

The United States shared the UK's lack of enthusiasm for large-scale technical and tactical development of armoured warfare in the 1920s and 1930s. During the late 1930s, however, the rapid worsening of world affairs prompted a re-evaluation of the situation. As previously mentioned, in the 1930s the US Army had sought to mitigate the worst effects of the USA's isolationist foreign policy and its lack of financing for the services, by pursuing an adventurous design philosophy with limited production allocated to industrial concerns capable of rapid expansion in times of need. This policy helped to keep the US Army abreast of overseas developments up to the mid-1930s, and the organization of the army's tank arm was also modified to consolidate tactical thinking.

The Churchill Crocodile was a conversion from the Churchill VII gun tank standard, with a flame gun installed in the forward part of the hull was supplied with 400 Imp gal (1,818 litres) of fuel from a two-wheel armoured tanker towed behind the vehicle by a quick-release mechanism. The fuel was forced to the flame gun by compressed nitrogen carried in five bottles in the trailer: flame could be projected to a typical range of 80yds (73m) and a maximum range of 120yds (110m).

The main tank types in service with the Armored Force in 1941 were the Light Tank M3 and the Medium Tank M3, both introduced to service in that year after standardization in 1940. The Light Tank M3 was a straightforward development of the Light Tank M2A4, which had been standardized in 1939 as the final expression of the basic concept pioneered in the M2A1 of 1935. The Americans had wished to develop a more capable light tank, perhaps armed with a 75mm (2.95in) main gun, but the need to undertake development as rapidly as possible to match potential enemies' numerical superiority necessitated an M2 update rather than a new vehicle; this removed any possibility of a larger-calibre main gun because of the M2's narrow hull, itself dictated by the width capability of the Engineer Corps' pontoon bridging equipment.

The M2A4 was a moderately useful machine. Its mobility and firepower were considered adequate, but there was concern about the level of protection provided by the riveted plate armour: overall thickness was satisfactory, but serious reservations were expressed about the protection offered against air attack, which the opening operations of World War II had shown to be considerably more devastating than had been expected. Thus the M2 was taken in hand for development with thicker armour on the upper surfaces, although the overall level of protection was improved by the adoption of reliable homogeneous armour rather than the brittle face-hardened armour of the M2 series. This improved armour was used for the all-riveted construction of the baseline M3A1, raising weight from the M2A4's 11.685 tonnes to 12.50 tonnes in the M3A1, standardized in July 1940.

Production of the M3 series continued until August 1942, the American Car and Foundry Company delivering some 5,811 M3 tanks in just over two years. The Americans failed to fall into the trap of three- rather than four-man crews, and the M3's complement consisted of a driver, assistant driver/hull gunner, commander and gunner. The turret therefore had a crew of two, a situation ameliorated by the comparative light weight of the ammunition for the 37mm main gun, which did not impose too great a burden on the gunner. Apart from the 37mm M5 or M6 main gun, the M3A1's armament comprised five 0.3in (7.62mm) Browning machine-guns located as a single co-axial weapon, a single bow weapon, a single anti-aircraft weapon on the commander's fixed turret-roof cupola, and two weapons in side sponsons fixed to deliver forward fire, (these two weapons

The Churchill Ark was a ramp-type bridging tank: the turret was removed and the upper part of the hull revised as a 'roadway' with folding ramps at each end. The vehicle was driven into the gap to be bridged and the ramps were then lowered, creating an 'instant road' across which other vehicles could pass.

Designed for the creation of a pathway over which infantry and trucks could cross barbed wire or poor ground, the carpet-laying concept was used in several forms by variants of the Churchill infantry tank, which could carry a large bobbin of reinforced hessian material for rapid laying under the tank's tracks.

were often omitted, especially in British service where sand-shields were usually installed in place of the machine-guns).

The M3 series was widely used by the British and dominion forces, and was given the name General Stuart whilst in British service. The tank was widely admired for its high level of protection, reliability, high speed and good agility in difficult terrain, and this admiration was reflected in the nickname 'Honey', which was generally used in preference to the official British name. Total production of the Light Tank M3 series up to October 1943 amounted to 13,859 tanks, making this the most prolific light tank series of World War II. The type was extensively used in most Allied theatres and, due to features such as its stabilized gun, was still an effective weapon against Japanese tanks in 1945. What cannot be ignored, however, are the type's several limitations, most notably its high silhouette and angular lines, the latter contributing significantly to the creation of several shot traps.

The next stage in US light tank development was inspired by the car industry rather than the Ordnance Department. The Light Tank M5 was suggested by Cadillac, which proposed to a sceptical Ordnance Department that the M3 could be revised without difficulty to accept a different powerplant and transmission: the powerplant would be a pair of Cadillac V-8 car engines, and the transmission the Cadillac Hydra-Matic automatic type. Cadillac converted an M3 to this standard as the M3E2. The conversion was completed in October 1941, and the revised model was standardized in February 1942 as the Light Tank M5 with a welded hull and the hull front thickened to a maximum of 64mm (2.5in). The turret was that of the M3A1, and the model weighed 14.97 tonnes with 220hp (164kW) available from the ganged Cadillac engines. The M5 was named the General Stuart VI by the British, and was succeeded in production from September 1942 by the M5A1 (also called the General Stuart VI). This final version weighed 15.38 tonnes, and differed from the M5 in having the turret of the M3A3 with radio bulge, improved main gun mounting, larger hatches for the driver and co-driver, and an escape hatch in the belly. Production of the M5 series amounted to 8,884 (2,074 M5s and 6,810 M5A1s) before production terminated in October 1944.

Designed from 1933 to meet a French army requirement for a light infantry support tank, the Renault Type ZM (otherwise known as the Char Léger R-35) was a two-man type weighing 10 tons and armed with a 37mm short-barrel gun in a small hand-operated turret. Some 2,000 were built for the French army, whose most important tank it was in 1940, and the type was also exported to Poland, Romania, Turkey and Yugoslavia.

Unofficially known as the CV35 and more formally as the Carro Veloce 33/II, this was a simple and generally ineffective tankette with an armament of two 0.303in (7.7mm) machine-guns in the front of the 'fighting compartment'.

The next US light tank to enter large-scale production was the result of a carefully planned programme designed to yield a high-quality successor to the M3 and M5 series. This was the Light Tank M24, which emerged as the best light tank of World War II: firepower was superior to that of all medium tanks of 1939 through the use of a lightweight 75mm (2.95in) T13E1 gun with concentric recoil mechanism derived from the M5 aircraft weapon; protection was provided by a considerable lowering of silhouette combined with careful design of thinner (and lighter) armour, offering a high level of ballistic protection with few shot traps; and mobility was at least equal to that of the highly praised M5.

Launched in April 1943, the programme that led to the M24 incorporated the engine and transmission that had proved so successful in the M5, and the running gear of the 76mm Gun Motor Carriage M18 'Hellcat', a high-mobility tank destroyer using torsion bar suspension for five medium-diameter road wheels on each side. Such a vehicle was proposed by the Cadillac Motor Car Division of the General Motors Corporation, and two prototypes were ordered under the designation Light Tank T24. These were delivered in October 1943, and proved so successful during initial running trials that 1,000 were ordered even before the full service trials had begun. The tank was standardized as the Light Tank M24 in July 1944, and production orders eventually totalled 5,000 units, of which 4,070 had been built by June 1945. The M24 entered service with the US Army in 1944, and in 1945 a small quantity was supplied to the British army, which gave the name Chaffee to the type.

The US Army expended enormous development and production effort on medium tanks, which were the mainstay of the service's armoured divisions in World War II. In the late 1930s the US Army's principal vehicles in this class were the Medium Tank M2, and the similar M2A1 armed with a 37mm main gun, but in 1940 it was realized that despite their recent development, these machines were obsolete by the standard now set by German tank development and operations. In August 1940, therefore, the heads of the Armored Force and Ordnance Department decided on the specification for a new medium tank with armour on a 38mm (1.5in) basis and a 75mm (2.95in) main gun. So far as these features were concerned the specification was adequate: problems arose with the realization that the US Army had lagged behind the European nations in developing large-diameter turrets of the type required for a 75mm (2.95in) gun, and that an alternative installation would have to be considered. It was decided, therefore, to upgrade the M2 as the new Medium Tank M3, with thicker armour and a 75mm (2.95in) sponson-mounted gun in addition to the existing 37mm weapon (in a cast rather than welded turret surmounted by a secondary turret accommodating the commander and a 0.3in/7.62mm machine-gun). Late in August 1940 a recently placed order for 1,000 M2A1s was modified to the same number of M3s.

The key to the new tank was the M2 gun, which was in fact an interim model, the definitive weapon in this calibre being the M3 which was ready for installation on later M3 tanks, and was also earmarked for the M3's successor, the legendary M4. The primary limitation of the 75mm (2.95in) gun mounting in the M3 was its small traverse in its casemate, while a useful feature was the provision (for the first time in an operational tank) of a Westinghouse stabilization system for the main and secondary guns in elevation: this allowed moderately accurate fire even with the tank on the move, a feature impossible with previous shoulder- or gear-controlled guns. In tactical terms, the location of the main gun in a sponson meant that much of the tank's considerable height had to be exposed in order to bring the gun into action, while the engagement of targets more than a small angle off the centreline involved manoeuvring the whole vehicle.

Built only in prototype form, the SOMUA Sav 40 was a 2.75in (75mm) self-propelled gun based on the S-35 medium tank.

The Strv 33, otherwise known as the Strv m/40 L, was the first tank of Swedish design to enter full production, an event that took place in 1940. This three-man type was a 9.5 ton light tank armed with a 37mm gun, and among its advanced features was a pre-selector gearbox.

Prototypes of the new M3 were delivered in January 1941 by Chrysler, additional vehicles following from American Locomotive (Alco) and Baldwin by April. Production was launched in August 1941, and 6,258 M3s were built before production ceased in December 1942. The six-man M3 bore a marked similarity to the M2, retaining the massive and angular hull, the aero engine-derived powerplant, and the running gear. Curiously, given the fact that the 23.37 tonne M2A1 was powered by a 400hp (298kW) Wright radial engine, the 27.22 tonne M3 had only a 340hp (253.5kW) version of the same unit.

The M3 entered US service in 1941, and was also delivered in substantial numbers to the British, primarily for service in North Africa and the Far East. Although the M3 medium tank's production life was comparatively short, the appearance of several important variants reflected the rapid pace of development in the first half of World War II, and the ability of American manufacturing companies to respond to these developments.

The original M3 (General Lee I in British service) had a riveted hull and

A French medium tank, the SOMUA S-35 was one of the best tanks in the world at the time of introduction in the second half of the 1930s. This 20-ton vehicle was the first tank in the world with all-cast hull and turret construction, and with a crew of three was armed with a 47mm gun and co-axial 0.295in (7.5mm) machine-gun in an electrically traversed turret. Production totalled 500 tanks.

Right and below right: The American solution to the creation of a medium tank with a large-calibre gun, at a time when insufficient development had been undertaken of the appropriate turret and traverse mechanism, was the adoption of a 2.75in (75mm) gun in a casemated installation on the right-hand side of the hull. This resulted in the Medium Tank M3 that was known to the British as the General Lee: the main gun was installed in a cast casemate that allowed only limited traverse, requiring the whole tank to be slewed to achieve large changes in gun azimuth, and was complemented by a 37mm gun in a cast turret. The rest of the tank was of riveted construction changed in later variants to a riveted lower hull and cast upper hull, and finally to all-welded construction for greater integrity and reduced weight. The upper photograph is of the first M3, and the lower photograph shows an M3 off the production line. The six-man production model weighed 26.8 tons, and with a 340hp (253.5kW) Continental R-975 radial engine had a speed of 26mph (42km/h).

a Wright R-975 radial petrol engine, although some M3 (Diesel) tanks were fitted with a Guiberson T-1400 diesel engine to overcome shortages of the Wright engine. Next came the M3A1 (General Lee II), mechanically identical to the M3 with Wright or Guiberson engine, but built to the extent of 300 vehicles exclusively by Alco, the only company in the programme able to produce this variant's cast upper hull (whose side hatches were later eliminated to provide extra strength, an escape hatch then being added in the belly). The M3A2 was not used by the British, although the designation General Lee III had been allocated, and the variant was mechanically identical with the M3 but based on a welded rather than riveted hull. M3A2 production amounted to only 12 vehicles before Baldwin switched to the 28.58 tonne M3A3 (General Lee IV) with a welded hull and a completely revised powerplant. This powerplant comprised two General Motors 6-71 diesels coupled to deliver 375hp (280kW): the larger engine installation reduced fuel capacity, but the efficiency of the diesel powerplant boosted range. Baldwin's production totalled 322 vehicles, and some British-

operated M3A3s were re-engined with the Wright radial and given the designation General Lee V. The M3A4 (General Lee VI) was identical to the original M3 in everything but its engine, which was a 370hp (276kW) Chrysler A-57 multibank petrol unit made by combining five car cylinder blocks on a common crankshaft; the engine was longer than the earlier units, and to provide an adequate engine compartment, the hull had to be enlarged and the weight increased to 29.03 tonnes. Production of 109 vehicles was undertaken by Chrysler. The final production variant was the M3A5, identical to the M3A3 in every respect but its hull, which was riveted rather than welded for a weight of 29.03 tonnes, and had the side doors either welded shut or eliminated: Baldwin delivered 591 of these vehicles, the last of them with the longer M3 gun fitted with a counterbalance weight at the muzzle.

As mentioned earlier, tanks of the M3 series were delivered to the UK under Lend-Lease, and with the name General Lee. The British also bought a variant of the basic M3 with a number of modifications (the General Grant). The most notable of these modifications was to the 360-degree traverse turret, which was lengthened to the rear so that a radio could be installed, and stripped of its secondary turret to reduce overall height. Similar modification was later made to the M3A5 to produce the General Grant II, whereupon the original variant became the General Grant I. It was as the General Grant that the type made its combat debut in the Battle of Gazala in May 1942. Here for the first time the British had a tank with a gun matching that of the Germans' PzKpfw IV. The importance of the Lee/Grant to the British was considerable, and although there were problems with the fuses and filling of the type's HE shell earlier in 1942, the tank played a significant part in the British success at the second Battle of El Alamein in October and November 1942.

The M3 was of tactical importance in its own right, but was also significant in buying time for the development of the Americans' most important medium tank of World War II. It had been appreciated from the beginning of the M3 programme that the sponson-mounted main gun was a potent limitation, and on 29 August 1940 (just one day after the first production order for the M3 had been placed), design work began on an M3

Together with its Light Tank M5 successor with a different type of powerplant, the Light Tank M3 was built in very large numbers for the USA and also for a number of American allies.

successor with its 75mm (2.95in) main gun in a 360-degree traverse turret. This would in itself provide great tactical improvement, while elimination of the sponson reduced the volume requiring armour protection, thereby allowing a lighter weight of armour for a more sprightly vehicle or, more practically, greater weight of armour over the protected volume that now accommodated five rather than six men. As much as possible of the M3 was retained, and the result was the Medium Tank T6 development model with a short-barrel M2 gun in a cast turret on a cast hull. The machine weighed 30.48 tonnes, was powered by a 400hp (298kW) Wright radial engine, and in addition to its main gun possessed an armament of four 0.3in (7.62mm) machine-guns, located as one co-axial, one bow and two fixed forward-firing nose guns. Prototype vehicles were delivered in September 1941, and trials confirmed the expectations of the designers and the army. In October 1941, a slightly modified version of the T6 (with a belly hatch and an additional driver's hatch in place of the side doors) was standardized as the Medium Tank M4, better known by the name Sherman (bestowed initially by the British within their system of naming US tanks after famous American generals). The M4 was planned to supersede the M3 on all current medium tank production lines, with additional sources coming on stream as production tempo increased. It was then realized that adequate casting facilities were not available for the anticipated number of hulls (at one time planned as 2,000 vehicles per month), and a more box-like upper hull of welded construction was developed as an alternative. Vehicles with the welded hull were designated M4, and those with the cast hull M4A1: both used the same one-piece cast turret, which had a maximum frontal thickness of 76mm (3in), an Oilgear hydraulic or Westinghouse electric power traverse system, and a stabilization system for the main gun in elevation. The main gun was the longer-barreled M3 weapon rather than the M2 used in the T6 vehicle.

In overall layout the Sherman was typical of its era, with a forward compartment for the driver and co-driver/nose gunner (the two fixed guns of the T6 were abandoned soon after the M4A1 came into production), a

The Medium Tank M4 Sherman was never the equal of its better German opponents in qualitative terms, but was reliable and available in very large numbers to equip the US Army and several other armies.

central fighting compartment for the commander, gunner and loader, and a rear compartment for the engine. On each side the running gear comprised three twin-wheel bogies with vertical volute spring suspension, three track-return rollers – one located at the top of each bogie attachment unit ('first-type suspension'), a front drive sprocket and a rear idler. The standard engine was the 400hp (298kW) Wright R-975 radial petrol engine.

The Sherman ran through a large number of variants and subvariants, and these are listed below in order of designation rather than production by the M3 manufacturers, who included Federal Machine and Welder, Fisher Body, the Ford Motor Company, and Pacific Car and Foundry. First in the designation sequence was the M4, designated Sherman I by the British: 8,389 of this model were built, 6,748 of them with the standard 75mm (2.95in) M3 gun and 1,641 with the 105mm (4.13in) M4 howitzer in the close-support role; the British designated the latter version the Sherman IB, and the suffix 'B' was used thereafter to denote Shermans with the howitzer. The M4 was standardized in October 1941 but became only the third model to go into production, and was distinguishable by its all-welded hull.

Next in designation sequence, but actually the first to enter production, was the M4A1 (Sherman II in British terms) with a cast hull. During the course of production the M4A1 received differential and hull front modifications parallel to those of the M4, and the track-return rollers were later shifted to the rear of the bogie attachment units ('second-type suspension'). Like the M4, the combat weight was 30.16 tonnes. Production of this variant totalled 9,677, of which 6,281 were completed with the M3 gun and the other 3,396 with the 76.2mm (3in) M1 high-velocity gun, whose installation was signified in British terminology by the designation Sherman IIA. This gun resulted from the realization by both the Armored Force and the Ordnance Department that the M3 gun was relatively indifferent in armour-penetration capability by comparison with the guns of contemporary

Opposite: The Medium Tank M4 Sherman was based on the same basic chassis as the Medium Tank M3, and was built in a large number of variants with different main guns, a cast or welded hull, vertical volute suspension that was later replaced by horizontal volute suspension, and a wide assortment of engine types so that deliveries of this war-winning weapon were not delayed when production of the chassis and hull exceeded that of the original Continental R-975 radial engine.

Seen after being knocked out on the beach of Normandy in June 1944, this is a Sherman of the 'Crab' type in which power from the main engine rotated chain flails which struck the ground in front of the tank and thereby detonated any pressure-activated mines. The tank otherwise possessed full combat capability through retention of its standard turreted gun.

German tanks. Over two months, the M1 was evolved from an anti-aircraft weapon, and tested during September 1942 in a standard M4 turret. This proved too small for the more powerful weapon, which was then installed in the cylindrical turret designed for the 90mm (3.54in) gun of the Medium Tank T23. This turret proved excellent, and could be installed on the M4 without modification. The gun/turret combination was authorized for the M4A3 in February 1944, deliveries beginning in the following month; the gun/turret combination was also used on the M4, M4A1 and M4A2, all signified in British usage by the suffix 'A' after the roman mark number.

The M4A2 was called Sherman III or Sherman IIIA by the British, depending on armament, and after standardization in December 1941 became the second Sherman variant to enter production. This 31.30 tonne type was similar to the M4 with a welded hull, but had a different powerplant in the form of a 410hp (306kW) General Motors 6046 diesel engine, comprising two General Motors 6-71 diesels geared to a common propeller shaft. Production amounted to 11,283 tanks, 8,053 of them with the 75mm (2.95in) gun and 3,230 with the 76.2mm (3in) gun.

In January 1942 a new variant was standardized as the M4A3, designated Sherman IV by the British. This again was similar to the M4 with a welded hull, but was fitted with a custom-designed engine, the 500hp (373kW) Ford GAA. This powerful and reliable petrol unit was instrumental in making the M4A3 the single most important Sherman variant: 11,424 were built, 5,015 with the 75mm (2.95in) gun, 3,370 with the 76.2mm (3in) gun and the other 3,039 with the 105mm (4.13in) howitzer. Once the M4A3 was available, the Americans generally reserved this model for themselves and disbursed the types with other engines to their Lend-Lease allies.

The M4A4 (Sherman V) was the main type supplied to the UK. The type was standardized in February 1942 as an M4 variant with a 425hp (317kW) Chrysler multi-bank engine, created by marrying five car engine cylinder blocks to a common crank-case. This was the same engine as used in the M3A4, and required a lengthening of the rear hull and an additional four track shoes on each side. The type was phased out of production in September 1943, and all 7,499 examples had the 75mm (2.95in) gun.

The designation M4A5 was used in the United States for the Ram tank that was a Canadian-built derivative of the M4, so the next production Sherman was the M4A6, designated Sherman VII by the British. The type was standardized in October 1943, and may be considered a variant of the M4A4 with the 497hp (371kW) Caterpillar D-200A diesel engine: the longer hull, more widely spaced bogies, extended tracks and 32.21 tonne weight were retained, and the 75mm (2.95in) gun was standard. Production amounted to only 75 tanks, for at the end of 1943 it was decided to cease powerplant experimentation and concentrate all production effort on the Wright- and Ford-engined models. Total production of Sherman gun tanks was 48,347, but this is by no means the whole of the Sherman story (or even of the Sherman gun tank story), for there were a large number of important variants produced by production-line, depot or field modification.

The best known of these variants is perhaps the Sherman 'Firefly', a British conversion with the 17pdr (3in/76.2mm) high-velocity anti-tank gun (indicated by the suffix 'C') for enhanced tank-destroying capability. Most Fireflies were of the Sherman VC variety, but there were also Sherman IC, IIC, IIIC and IVC versions, and the family proved highly important in the Normandy and North-West European campaigns as the Allied tanks best able to tackle the Panther and Tiger on anything approaching equal firepower .

The importance of the M4 Sherman tank in the Allied victory of World War II cannot be overemphasized. The Sherman may not have been a

The most capable version of the Medium Tank M4 Sherman was a hybrid Anglo-American model, the Sherman Firefly that was a conversion of the M4A1 (Sherman II), M4A2 (Sherman III), M4A3 (Sherman IV) and M4A4 (Sherman V) with the standard American gun replaced by the British 17pdr anti-tank gun. This turned the basic Sherman, which was an indifferent anti-tank weapon, into a devastating killer of German tanks.

qualititive match for the best German tanks (it lacked the all-round fighting capabilities of the Panther, and was not as heavily armed and protected as the Tiger), but it was adequate to its tasks, and was produced in the vast numbers that allowed Allied tank formations to overwhelm the Germans and, to a lesser extent, the Japanese. The Sherman remained in widespread service into the 1970s, and is still used by a number of armies.

The last category of American tank to be discussed is the heavy tank, of which the only type to enter more than token US service was the T26, which had been designed as a medium tank but increased in weight to the point at which it had to be reclassified as a heavy tank (in June 1944). This vehicle was the culmination of a development programme that had encompassed the T20, T22, T23, T25 and T26 medium tanks in all their variations, and to avoid confusion the first heavy tank model was classified Heavy Tank T26E3 and standardized for limited procurement in November 1944. The T26 was subjected to intensive combat evaluation, and in January 1945 was declared battleworthy, leading to the type's standardization in March 1945 as the Heavy Tank M26 General Pershing. The M26 was considered the primary US tank in the armoured battles with the Germans' Tiger tanks, though experience in Europe confirmed that while the M26 was equal to the Tiger in protection and superior in mobility, it was decidedly inferior in firepower, where the German 88mm (3.46in)kWK 36 and 43 weapons reigned supreme.

There were a number of variants of the M26 in its basic gun tank role, and just as there was a 'Lightweight Combat Team' derived from the M24 Chaffee, there was a 'Heavyweight Combat Team' derived from the M26 Pershing. In the basic line of development as a gun tank, the M26 spawned five derivatives. The M26A1 was very similar to the M26 but had a revised M3A1 main gun with bore evacuator and single-baffle muzzle brake; some of the type were fitted with a system to stabilize the main gun in elevation. The M26E1 was the basic vehicle fitted with the 90mm (3.54in) T54 gun: this had a concentric recoil system and used fixed rather than separate-loading ammunition, requiring the ammunition stowage inside the tank to be revised. The T26E2 was a close-support version with a 105mm (4.13in) howitzer as stabilized main armament; in July 1945 the T26E2 was standardized for limited production as the M45. The T26E4 was also very similar to the M26 but had a 90mm (3.54 in) T15E2 gun in place of the M26's

Built only in small numbers, the Cruiser Tank Ram was a Canadian effort to combine what was best in American and British tank thinking and to create a vehicle suitable for production in Canada. The Ram Mk I therefore combined the chassis, engine, transmission and trackwork of the Medium Tank M3, a cast upper hull and turret of Canadian design and manufacture, and British main armament in the form of the 2pdr (40mm) main gun. Production amounted to 50 vehicles between 1941 and 1943, but these were used only for training and were superseded from 1942 by the Ram Mk II (illustrated) with a number of improvements including a 6pdr (57mm) main gun. Production of the Ram Mk II totalled 1,899 vehicles.

M3 of the same calibre. And the T26E5 was the heavy tank counterpart to the M4A3E2 'Jumbo', a dedicated assault version with the frontal armour thickened to a maximum of 279mm (11in) on the mantlet, 190.5mm (7.5in) on the turret and 152mm (6in) on the hull, increasing weight to 46.27 tonnes; production amounted to only 27 vehicles.

Production of the M26 totalled 2,432, but the type saw only limited service in World War II. In May 1946 it was reclassified as a medium tank once again, and served with considerable distinction in the Korean War (1950-53). The Pershing marked a decisive turning point in the design of American medium tanks: namely the culmination of the evolutionary design process from the M2 series, yet its divergence from the main sequence in terms of its large road wheels, torsion bar suspension, hull-mounted track-return rollers and rear drive sprockets heralded the beginning of the post-World War II series of medium and battle tanks, from the M47 to the M60.

Seen during the course of desert manoeuvres, the Light Tank M5 was standardised in February 1942 as a development of the Light Tank M3 with a powerplant of two Cadillac car engines driving an automatic transmission.

American tanks made an enormous contribution to the Allied victory in World War II. The Americans themselves fielded large numbers of armoured divisions and independent tank battalions – and also provided their allies with enormous numbers of tanks. The hallmarks of the American tanks were initially their availability, reliability and comparatively heavy armament. And as the war progressed, the capabilities of American tank designers and the vast industrial machine that supported them combined to develop better designs that were put into production without hampering the flow of existing designs.

The nation that stands out as the most important exponent of armoured warfare in World War II, however, must be the USSR. The Soviets had devoted their energies in the 1920s and early 1930s to absorbing as much imported technology as possible, while at the same time pursuing a policy of limited indigenous development. By the mid-1930s the Soviets had built up a considerable armoured force, backed by a substantial industrial machine capable of supporting and expanding the in-service tank fleet. In the later 1930s the Soviets consciously turned away from their policy of mass production, and concentrated on the development of tanks that were qualitatively equal or superior to the best of Western tanks, but which could still be manufactured in large numbers.

At the beginning of World War II, the Soviets were undertaking a complete overhaul of their tank fleet, with the development and introduction of a new generation to replace the derivative designs of the 1930s. Given the geographical nature of the USSR, with its poor road and rail communications over vast areas indented by large rivers and split by extensive marshes, it was inevitable that the Soviets would place great emphasis for reconnaissance on the light tank, which should preferably be an amphibious type. In the late 1930s the most important in-service types were the T-27, T-37A and T-38, and to replace these the two-man T-40 light amphibious tank was developed, its prototype appearing in 1936: this resembled the BT-IS in overall configuration, and was a complete departure from earlier Soviet light tank designs in its welded construction,

The final expression of American thinking about heavy tanks in World War II was the M26 General Pershing that was used in limited numbers during the final stages of the war against Germany. After the end of the war the type was reclassified as a medium tank, and became a mainstay of the US armoured forces until the mid-1950s. This is an M26 in the Korean War.

independent torsion bar suspension for the arrangement of four road wheels on each side, and truncated conical turret accommodating the commander and the armament of one 12.7mm (0.5in) and one 7.62mm (0.3in) co-axial machine-gun. Standard components were used wherever possible, as in the 85hp (63.3kW) GAZ-202 petrol engine, and the type was buoyant without aid, being propelled in the water by a single propeller. Weight was 5.59 tonnes with a maximum armour thickness of 13mm (0.51in). The original T-40 had a blunt nose, but the later T-40A had a more streamlined nose, and the non-amphibious T-40S of 1942 had slightly thicker armour and provision for a 20mm main gun. The T-40 series served from 1941 to 1946.

The T-40 was planned for only modest service as the Soviets envisaged that the T-60 light tank should supplement and then supplant all in-service light tanks from 1942. Design of this vehicle was already in hand when the lessons of the Germans' 1941 invasion became understood. These suggested that the primary requirement of the light tank should not be mobility (including amphibious capability) to the exclusion of firepower and protection, but rather a more judicious blend of all three components. The design of the two-man T-60 was therefore revised to produce a more capable machine of all-welded construction with thicker armour and greater firepower. The Soviets had hoped to instal a 37mm gun, but the recoil forces of this weapon could not be absorbed by the small turret ring: in its place the designers fitted the exceptional 20mm ShVAK cannon, and a 7.62mm (0.3in) machine-gun was installed co-axially. The T-60 entered production in November 1941, and nearly 6,000 were built before the type was superseded in production by the T-70 light tank during 1943. The T-60 weighed 5.15 tonnes and was powered by an 85hp (63.3kW) GAZ-202 petrol, and its only tank variant was the T-60A of 1942 with thicker frontal armour and solid

The Soviet heavy tank mainstay at the time of the Germans' June 1941 invasion of the USSR, the KV-1 was based closely on the design of the T-100 and SMK heavy tanks with these two vehicles' forward turret removed and the tall barbette carrying the superfiring main turret eliminated to create a considerably more effective tank. The KV-1 was well protected, and its armament comprised one 3in (7.62mm) main gun and three machine-guns. The 46.35-ton vehicle had a crew of five and was powered by a 550hp (410kW) diesel engine for a speed of 22mph (35km/h).

The M24 Chaffee was the final expression of American light tank thinking in World War II, and was an exceptional vehicle of its type with well-disposed and well-sloped armour, a moderately powerful gun, and very good combination of performance and agility.

rather than spoked road wheels, although after the introduction of the T-70, surplus T-60s were converted as mountings for Katyusha rockets or as tractors for 57mm anti-tank guns.

Despite its improvement over the T-40 in firepower and protection, the T-60 was soon found to be inadequate in these respects for the military requirements of the Eastern Front. The replacement was the T-70 light tank, which retained the basic chassis of the T-60, but with the drive sprockets shifted from the rear to the front and the armour revised in shape and angle to generate better protection. The modified turret still accommodated a single, tactically overtaxed commander/gunner/loader: this one man had to command the tank and operate the armament of one 45mm L/46 high-velocity gun and one 7.62mm (0.3in) co-axial machine-gun. The T-70 weighed 9.96 tonnes but had better performance than its predecessor due to improved runnning gear and a powerplant of two 70hp (52.2kW) ZIS-202 petrol engines. Production of the T-70 started late in 1941, and ended in the autumn of 1943 after the delivery of 8,225 vehicles, including the improved T-70A with thicker armour.

The core of the Soviets' armoured thinking was the medium tank, and in this category was the legendary T-34, which was acknowledged as the most important tank of World War II, and was arguably the most influential tank ever developed. By Western standards the tank was mechanically unsophisticated, with its four-speed gearbox and clutch/brake steering, but the power train and running gear/suspension were ruthlessly reliable, the armament formidable, and the protection far superior to that of the German PzKpfw IV tank. Small-scale encounters with the T-34 units were recorded by the Germans as early as June 1941, and fully operational T-34 units appeared with increasing frequency in the autumn of the same year. The advent of the T-34 was an enormous and thoroughly unpleasant surprise to the Germans: up to this point in World War II, their Panzer divisions had enjoyed an unequalled blend of tactical superiority and technical advantage; from this time the Germans' technical edge was eroded, and their tactical expertise was slowly matched by the Soviets.

The T-34 (often called the T-34/76 in Western terminology for the calibre of its main gun) appeared in prototype form at the end of 1939 for exhaustive evaluation and proving trials in the first six months of 1940. The T-34/76 was a further development of the T-32 prototype vehicle with a number of detail modifications, and slightly thicker protection on the least protected areas for a weight of 26.725 tonnes. The hull and turret were of welded construction, and the type was powered by a 500hp (373kW) diesel engine.

The hull was sectioned into three compartments. The forward compartment provided side-by-side seating for the driver and bow machine-gunner, who doubled as radio operator in the company and platoon commanders' vehicles that were the only tanks fitted with this equipment. The fighting compartment was just behind the short forward compartment rather than in the centre, and the engine compartment was at the rear. The transmission to the rear drive sprockets was also located in the rear compartment, and proved the least reliable single component of the T-34. The least successful tactical feature of the T-34/76 in its initial form was the turret, a small unit with manual or electric traverse. Mounted co-axially with the main armament was a 7.62mm (0.3in) DT machine-gun, and the bow machine-gun was a similar weapon.

The T-34/76 entered production in the middle of 1940, and although exact figures are not available, year totals seem to have been in the order of 115 machines in 1940, 2,800 in 1941, 5,000 in 1942, 10,000 in 1943, 11,750 in 1944 and 10,000 in 1945, giving a grand total of about 39,665 T-34s of all types.

The first production variant had the Western designation T-34/76A, and was the version described above with a welded turret carrying the Model 1939 L11 main gun. The welded turret was somewhat complex to build, and as the Soviets possessed good capability for the production of large castings a cast turret (still with the same L/30.5 gun in a rolled plate mounting) was introduced to allow turret production to match the steadily increasing tempo of hull production. During 1941, the Germans began to field an increasing number of 50mm PaK 38 anti-tank guns whose projectiles could pierce the T-34's armour at short ranges, and in response the Soviets increased the thickness of the T-34's frontal armour. In 1942 the Soviets introduced to the T-34 series the improved Model 1940 F34 gun with a longer barrel, a weapon that had been pioneered in the 1930s for the T-28 and T-35 tanks. This Soviet gun compared favourably with the 75mm (2.95in)kWK L/24 and kWK 40 L/43 weapons carried by the Germans' contemporary PzKpfw IV tanks, but the T-34 still scored decisively over its German adversaries in protection, range and cross-country performance.

Throughout its history, the USSR placed considerable emphasis on evolutionary development of proved designs for ease of manufacture, reduced spares holding requirements, and simplification of training. Thus clear links to earlier battle tank types can be found in the T-54, which first appeared in 1947 as a development of the T-44, which itself was a 1944 prototype that drew extensively on the T-34 that was the Soviets' primary medium tank of World War II.

Seen in the form of a vehicle operated by the Finnish army, the T-55 was a simple development of the T-54 and first appeared in 1960 with a number of detail improvements and other major enhancements, such as a more powerful engine and the same 3.94in (100mm) main gun now in a stabilised mounting and provided with a greater quantity of ammunition.

The use of the longer 76.2mm (3in) gun in the T-34 is signalled in Western terminology by the designation T-34/76B, and T-34/76Bs are associated with welded as well as cast turrets. Thicker armour and the cast turret increased the T-34/76B's weight to 28.50 tonnes without any serious degradation of performance.

Some criticism had been levelled at the provision of a single large forward-hingeing hatch in the turret roof of these first models, and this deficiency was remedied in the T-34/76C that began to appear in 1943. This variant had twin hatches, which slightly increased overall height, and weight was boosted to 30.50 tonnes with a consequent decrease in speed. Other features of the T-34/76C were spudded tracks, improved vision devices and an armoured sleeve for the bow machine-gun.

By the time the T-34/76C was beginning to enter service, the Soviets were well advanced with the development of the up-gunned T-34/85 version, but saw considerable merit in maintaining the combat capability of the T-34/76 series with a number of improved features. The first of these was a revised hexagonal turret with a wider gun mounting/mantlet in a version known to the West as the T-34/76D: the new turret provided greater internal volume and, perhaps just as significant, removed the earlier turrets' rear overhang, whose slight horizontal separation from the rear decking had given German assault pioneers an ideal spot for the placement of anti-tank mines. The new turret increased tank weight to 31.40 tonnes, and another feature introduced on this variant (and retrofitted without delay on earlier marks) was provision for jettisonable external fuel tanks to increase the T-34/76's already considerable range. The T-34/76E was basically similar, but had a welded turret complete with a commander's cupola. The final T-34/76F had a cast turret with the commander's cupola, and also introduced a five-speed gearbox; only very limited production was undertaken before the T-34/76 series was superseded by the T-34/85.

The T-34/85 appeared in the autumn of 1943, with the new 85mm (3.35in) gun designated initially as the D-5T85, or in upgraded form as the ZIS-S53; the gun was used with a turret adapted from that of the KV-85 heavy tank. With either of these weapons the T-34/85 was a devastating tank, completely outclassing the PzKpfw IV and providing a match for the Panther and Tiger in all but outright firepower at medium and long ranges. The main gun was backed by two 7.62mm (0.3in) machine-guns (one bow and the other co-axial). The larger turret had the considerable advantage of allowing a tactical crew of three, the availability of a gunner and loader permitting the commander to concentrate on his primary function.

The T-34/85 was authorized for production in December 1943, and 283 had been built by the end of the year. By the end of 1944 some 11,000 T-34/85s had been delivered, and production continued into the post-war period: the type served with the Soviet armies until the mid-1950s, and is still in use in many parts of the world.

The T-34 series was produced in greater numbers than any other tank in history, and formed the most important part of the Soviets' tank inventory in World War II. The success of the series did not prevent the Soviets from developing a successor in the form of the T-44, but as this was placed in production only after the end of the war as recursor of a new family of tanks, it is discussed below.

The Soviets were long-term advocates of the heavy tank, and during the 1930s they conceived the massive T-100 and SMK types, with their main turrets on barbettes to give them a superfiring capability over the auxiliary turret. The fallacy of this practice was fully revealed in the Russo-Finnish 'Winter War' (1939-40). Yet at the beginning of World War II the USSR

The affinity of the T-62 to the preceding T-54 and T-55 series is clear in the general configuration of the tank and in the ballistic shaping of the turret, but major changes were the longer and wider hull, the improved shaping of the turret, and the use of a larger-calibre 4.53in (115mm) main gun.

was the only country to have placed such monsters into full-scale production, the initial type being the KV-1, named after Klimenti Voroshilov. Design of the KV-1 began during February 1939 at the Kirov factory in Leningrad, the intention of the design team being a heavy tank less tall than its predecessors, and therefore overcoming their stability and visibility problems. The KV-1 was modelled on the T-100 and SMK (especially in the design and structure of the hull, and the nature of the running gear with torsion bar suspension), but excluded the auxiliary turret and its 45mm gun, thereby removing the need for the main turret's barbette and allowing a general reduction in overall dimensions and weight.

The prototype KV-1 was built between April and September 1939, and ordered into production in December, at the same time as the T-34 medium

Soviet Tank Philosophy

THROUGHOUT its existence, the Soviet Union worked to a single main principle for the design of the weapons used by its armed forces: a basic simplicity of core design that yet possessed the capability for considerable evolutionary development in the course of protracted production and service lives. This policy, so different from the 'gold plating' tendency of the Western nations in general and the USA in particular, meant that a weapon could be designed for its specific purpose with adequate volume for vital equipment but no provision for 'frills', and this translated into a thoroughly utilitarian weapon in which particular attention was paid to features such as reliability, high performance and, in the case of a tank, good protection and a large-calibre main gun provided with a large number of rounds.

Habitability came well down the designers' list of priorities, and although it has been argued in Western circles that this lack of 'comfort' soon began to degrade the capabilities of Soviet tank crews, it should be realized that such tank crews were used to conditions considerably more spartan than those of their Western counterparts and they were therefore better able to cope with the lack of creature comforts typical of Soviet armoured fighting vehicles.

The basic simplicity of Soviet tanks facilitated mass production at a rapid rate, eased the task of training crews with only modest technical skills, and also made less troublesome the task of upgrading the tanks as new generations of equipment became available. This should not be construed, however, to mean that the Soviets paid no attention to the safety of their tanks and their crews, for the Soviet authorities fully appreciated the investment that had been made in men and equipment. Thus Soviet tanks were generally notable for their good armour protection both in terms of thickness and inclination, their use from the late 1930s of a diesel engine running on low-volatility fuel for reduced fire hazard in combat as well as greater range on a given volume of fuel, and their use of a main gun generally one step up in calibre from that used by most of their Western contemporaries.

tank. The machine had a crew of five, a weight of 47.50 tonnes and a powerplant of one 600hp (447kW) V-2K diesel engine. The massive turret was made of welded armour between 30mm and 75mm (1.18in and 2.95in) thick with a 25mm (0.98in) cast mantlet, and was fitted with the same main armament as the T-34/76; the secondary armament comprised three 7.62mm (0.3in) machine-guns.

The KV-1 entered production in February 1940, and 245 had been produced by the end of the year. A few were sent for operational evaluation in the Finnish campaign, proving successful in the breakthrough of the Finns' Mannerheim Line defences. After the German invasion, the Kirov factory was evacuated to Chelyabinsk, in whose Tankograd all subsequent production was undertaken, to the extent of 13,500 chassis used for assault guns and heavy tanks. Variants of the KV-1 were the KV-1A of 1940 with the L/41.2 main gun, resilient road wheels and thicker frontal armour; the KV-1B of 1941 with even thicker frontal and lateral armour and later with a cast turret, increasing weight to 48.775 tonnes; the KV-1C of 1942 with the cast turret, wider tracks, an uprated engine and maximum armour thicknesses increased to 130mm (5.12in) on the hull and 120mm (4.72in) on the turret; and the KV-1s (skorostnoy, or fast) of 1942 with weight reduced to 43.185 tonnes by the omission of the appliqué armour used on the previous models.

The ultimate development of the Soviet heavy tank was the Iosef Stalin (IS, sometimes rendered JS) series, initially conceived to counteract the German development of new tank types with heavy protection and powerful armament. It was appreciated by the Soviets that their current service and development tanks might not be able to cope with these new German tanks, and early in 1943 a novel IS series was planned at the Kirov factory. Design was entrusted to the KV team, who used features of the KV series to reduce technical risk and to speed the design and development programme. Weight no greater than that of the KV was demanded, and as initial plans called for an 85mm (3.35in) main gun the designation IS-85 was allocated. The first of three prototypes appeared in the autumn of 1943, and although clearly derived from the KV series in its hull, powerplant and running gear, it was an altogether more formidable machine with highly sloped armour that was also extremelythick; hull armour was welded while the turret was the same cast unit as fitted on the KV-85. By comparison with the KV-85, the hull of the IS-85 had lower running gear to permit the use of a superstructure that overhung the tracks and allowed a larger turret ring. The care taken in component as well as overall design is indicated by the fact that the IS-85 emerged with 50mm (1.98in) more armour than the KV-85 but weighed some 2.00 tonnes less, allowing a higher maximum speed on a less powerful engine. It is believed that the IS-85 saw very limited operational service as the IS-1.

It was considered inappropriate for a heavy tank to have the same armament as the current medium tank, so it was proposed that a variant should be developed as the IS-100 with a 100mm (3.94in) main gun, in a process made very straightforward by the initial adoption of a large turret ring. A small number of IS-100 tanks were evaluated, but the type proceeded no further as an even more formidable machine had been proposed, with a new turret of superior ballistic shape and fitted with the 122mm (4.8in) D-25 gun. After development as the IS-122, the type was placed in production as the IS-2, and the considerably more potent turret/armament combination was also retrofitted to the small number of IS-100s that had been built to create the variant known in the West as the IS-1B, the original IS-1 being redesignated IS-1A to avoid confusion. The IS-2 was accepted for production at the end of October 1943 after an extremely rapid development programme, and by the end of the year some 100 IS-2 tanks had been delivered.

The Post-War Years

AFTER World War II, the victorious Allies undertook an intensive analysis of armoured warfare, especially the German technical research into all aspects of tank technology. The Soviets were content with the tactical and technical performance of their armoured forces in the last two years of the war, but the Western Allies had cause for considerable revision in their thinking, although there were many good features that could be retained for future development.

World War II had nearly bankrupted the UK, and the vast demobilization after the end of the war forced economies on the army and further straitened the situation at home. This position was worsened after 1947, when the grant of independence to India signalled the start of a rapid dissolution of the British empire: the departure of India removed the need for many of the imperial 'way stations' on the sea and air routes to the old viceroyalty, and after about 15 years, the British empires in Africa, the Near East, Middle East and Far East had disappeared, further reducing the UK's need for a large military capability. This capability had demanded a high-quality regular army supported by a territorial force, designed for high levels of strategic mobility so that any threat could be met by adequate strength and with minimum delay. The dissolution of the empire led to a reassessment of the role of the British army, the inevitable conclusion being that while the dwindling imperial commitment had still to be met, the new role of the army was in Europe as part of the NATO alliance. Like the imperial role, this demanded a modest but high-quality army, fielding the best of heavy weapons rather than ordnance designed for use against an unsophisticated enemy. The anticipated foe was now the USSR, and the vast tank fleet mustered and constantly improved by the Soviets represented a serious threat.

After the end of World War II the Heavy Tank M26 was reclassified as the Medium Tank M26, and further development at this time resulted in the M46. These two types were the US Army's standard battle tanks at the time of the Korean War, and further work on the M46 resulted in the M47 Patton, which was the chassis and hull of the M46 combined with the new turret and 3.54in (90mm) gun designed for the new T42 battle tank that was not yet ready for production. The M47 was essentially an interim type, although a very good one and a type that is still in limited service with a number of Third-world armies. As soon at it had entered production, work started on the development of a successor, which was basically the turret and main gun of the M47 combined with a new chassis and hull to create the M48 Patton. This entered service with the US Army in 1953, and remained in service with this force until superseded by the M60 that was in essence the M48 revised with a 4.13in (105mm) main gun. This is an M48 operating in Cambodia in the early 1970s.

Armed with a 2.95in (75mm) main gun, the M24 Chaffee had considerable firepower for a light tank.

The light tank concept had fallen out of favour with the British during World War II, and in the period immediately after the war the reconnaissance role was entrusted to wheeled scout cars and wheeled armoured cars. In the short term, and so far as tracked vehicles were concerned, the British kept in service the best of the cruiser and infantry tanks of World War II while working on replacements. These two types were the A41 Cruiser Tank Centurion and the A45 Infantry Tank Conqueror, both launched on their development careers in 1944.

After basic formulation by the Department of Tank Design in 1943, the A41 was entrusted to AEC for detail design with the object of producing a high-mobility cruiser tank characterized by improved Horstmann suspension, better protection through the adoption of thicker and better-sloped armour, and heavier firepower through the use of the 17pdr (76.2mm/3in) high-velocity gun in a mounting that would be readily adaptable to larger-calibre weapons; the secondary armament was also increased in the prototypes to a 20mm Polsten co-axial cannon, but it was eventually decided to revert to the standard 7.92mm (0.31in) Besa machine-gun, which was then replaced by a 0.3in (7.62mm) Browning machine-gun. Not included in the original concept were high road speed or anything more than minimal range, and these two factors were to be the Centurion's main limitations throughout its highly successful and lengthy service career.

Production of the Centurion was entrusted to the Royal Ordnance Factory in Leeds, Vickers-Armstrongs at Elswick and Leyland Motors at

All the British experience in armoured warfare during the course of World War II was used in the creation of the A41 Centurion battle tank, which remains one of the classic armoured fighting vehicles of the period after World War II with a good record of combat success in several wars. Illustrated here are Centurion Mk 5 tanks in which the problem of the earlier models' acute shortage of range was addressed by provision for an armoured monowheel trailer carrying additional fuel. The Centurion Mk 5 was also armed with a 20pdr (3.28in/83.4mm) main gun in place of the earlier models' 17pdr (3in/76.2mm) gun.

Leyland: by the time Centurion production ended in 1962, these companies had built over 4,400 of the series, including about 2,500 for export to countries such as Australia, Canada, Denmark, India, Iraq, Israel, Jordan, Kuwait, Lebanon, the Netherlands, South Africa, Sweden and Switzerland. The type is still in service with several of these countries, and is still being upgraded to maintain it as a viable weapon with a better fire-control system, modern armament and (in many cases) a diesel powerplant. Although limited in speed and range, the Centurion has proved to be a remarkably long-lived weapon because of its capability for up-armouring and up-gunning.

Six prototypes were completed before the end of World War II, but although these were shipped to Germany they arrived too late for combat. An extended period of development followed World War II as the concept of a battlefield team of cruiser and infantry tanks faded in face of the notion of the single battle tank that could undertake both halves of what was becoming a unified role, and the initial Centurion Mk 1 entered service in 1949 with a main armament of one 17pdr (76.2mm/3in) Tank Gun Mk 3, a considerably more powerful weapon than the 17pdr Tank Gun Mk 2 used in the Sherman 'Firefly', and radically more devastating than the slightly shorter 77mm Tank Gun Mk 2 used in the Comet.

Further development of the baseline model produced the Centurion Mk 2 with improved armour, but a major change came with the Centurion Mk 3, armed with the 20pdr (83.4mm/3.28in) Tank Gun Mk 1 offering still greater armour-penetrating capability. The Centurion Mk 4 was to have been the close-support counterpart of the Mk 3 with a 3.7in (94mm) Tank Howitzer Mk 1, but was not built, so the next production variant was the Centurion Mk 5, which was the first definitive version. It was a Vickers-designed counterpart to the Mk 3 vehicles, which were all brought up to this operationally improved standard. Further development produced the up-armoured Centurion Mk 5/1, and the Centurion Mk 5/2 which entered service in 1959 and was armed with the magnificent 105mm (4.13in) Tank Gun L7, a product of the Royal Ordnance Factories, fitted in a mounting that provided full stabilization in elevation to complement the turret's stabilization in azimuth.

The Centurion was probably produced in more variants than any other tank in the period after World War II, and after the Mk 5 variants, the sequence continued with the Centurion Mk 6, which was the Mk 5/2 up-armoured and fitted with additional fuel tankage; subvariants of the Mk 6 were the Centurion Mk 6/1 with a stowage basket on the turret rear and infra-red equipment to provide a limited night-driving and night-fighting capability, and the Centurion Mk 6/2 which introduced a ranging machine-gun for the main armament. The Centurion Mk 7 was a Leyland model with the 20pdr (83.4mm/3.28in) gun fitted with a fume extractor, and which was subsequently designed FV4007 in the Fighting Vehicle designation system; subvariants of the Mk 7 were the Centurion Mk 7/1 (FV4012) with improved armour, and the Centurion Mk 7/2 with the L7 gun. The Centurion Mk 8 was essentially the Mk 7 with a revised gun mounting, contra-rotating commander's cupola and provision for the commander's twin hatch covers to be raised for overhead protection when the commander's torso was out of the turret; subvariants of the Mk 8 were the Centurion Mk 8/1 with improved armour, and the Centurion Mk 8/2 with the L7 gun. The Centurion Mk 9 (FV4015) was the Mk 7 with thicker armour and the L7 gun; subvariants of the Mk 9 were the Centurion Mk 9/1 with the stowage basket and infra-red vision devices, and the Centurion Mk 9/2 had the ranging machine-gun. Following this was the Centurion Mk 10 (FV4017), essentially

Armour Penetration

THE initial solution to the task of penetrating enemy tanks' armour protection was the use of kinetic energy, in the form of a solid shot fired at high velocity to punch a hole through the armour or, failing that, to cause the inside of the armour to spall (flake into a large number of high-velocity fragments) and thereby wounding the crew.

Armour designers responded by toughening the armour and using it in thicker plates, and gun designers countered with denser shot fired at higher velocity. This see-saw battle between gun and armour designers continued into World War II, when the establishment of a plateau in gun and armour performance resulted in a switch to another means of offence in the form of the chemical-energy round.

This was developed during and after World War II in two basic forms as the HEAT and HESH rounds. In the HEAT (High Explosive Anti-Tank) round, a warhead with a specially shaped and copper-lined hollow in the forward edge of its explosive filling is detonated with as little spin as possible at precisely the optimum distance from the armour, the shaping of the explosive charge creating a jet of vaporised copper and very hot gases that burns its way through the armour to incinerate the crew and ignite the ammunition. in the HESH (High Explosive Squash Head) round, the warhead includes a mass of plastic explosive that is plastered onto the outside of the armour by the force of the impact, and then detonated to create a massive spall effect inside the tank.

The response of the armour designers was initially spaced armour, in which the force of the HEAT or HESH round's explosion is absorbed by an outer layer of armour separated by an air gap from the main armour that is therefore little affected, and then by composite armour in which a classified mix of metal, ceramics, fibrous matter and composite materials is used to make it difficult if not impossible for the explosive jet to find a path into the interior of the vehicle. The gun designer's response, already under development before the advent of composite armour, has been the kinetic-energy dart, which is made of dense material such as tungsten or depleted uranium, and fired from the main gun in bore-filling sabots that fall away as the projectile leaves the muzzle, allowing the small-diameter dart to travel to the target at extremely high velocity and punch a hole through the armour.

the Mk 8 with improved armour; subvariants of the Mk 10 were the Centurion Mk 10/1 with stowage basket and infra-red vision devices, and the Centurion Mk 10/2 with the ranging machine-gun. The Centurion Mk 11 was the Mk 6 with stowage basket, infra-red vision devices and ranging machine-gun, while the Centurion Mk 12 was the Mk 9 with the same improvements, and the final Centurion Mk 13 was the Mk 10 with infra-red vision devices and the ranging machine-gun.

The Centurion remains one of the classic tanks of all time, proving that the United Kingdom can produce a tank matching the best anywhere in the world. The same cannot be said of the A45, which was conceived as the Centurion's heavy companion and then planned as the baseline model in the Universal Tank series, which would have used the same hull for flamethrowing, dozing and amphibious variants. The A45 was not adopted, however, although its chassis became the core of a new heavy tank planned to tackle the IS-3 and its succesors in Soviet service. This was developed as the Conqueror (FV214), initial proof of concept being undertaken in a model called the Caernarvon (FV221), which was the hull of the Conqueror and the turret of the Centurion. The definitive Conqueror appeared in 1950, and the obsolescence of the concept that led to its development is indicated by the fact that production of only 180 vehicles was undertaken in the period between 1956 and 1959. Weighing 66.04 tonnes attributable mostly to very thick armour, the Conqueror was powered by the 810hp (604kW) Meteor 120 No. 2 Mk 1A petrol engine. It had a crew of four, and the massive cast turret accommodated a 120mm (4.72in) Tank Gun L11, one 0.3in (7.62mm) co-axial machine-gun and one 0.3in (7.62mm) machine-gun on the commander's cupola.

French tank developments had effectively ceased by June 1940, resuming only after the liberation of France had begun in 1944. Just before the fall of France, designers had completed preliminary work on the ARL-40, a project originated in 1938 for a Char B1 successor using the same hull

The M46 was in essence a product-improved M26, and was the first step in the evolutionary design process that provided the US Army's battle tanks from the M26 of World War II to the M60 that entered service in 1960 and is still in widespread service.

The M47 Patton is still in extensive service, many older vehicles having been upgraded for continued capability by the replacement of the original petrol engine with a diesel powerplant, revision of the suspension system, and replacement of the original 3.54in (90mm) main gun with a 4.13in (105mm) weapon. This is an M47 of the Italian army.

but with the 75mm (2.95in) gun located in a revolving turret rather than in a limited-traverse hull mounting. During the war the design was modified and modernized at the Atelier de Construction de Rueil (ARL) with different hull (retaining the Char B1's running gear and tracks), and a revised power-traversed Schneider turret accommodating a 90mm (3.54in) gun, and after the liberation this was placed in production as the Char de Transition ARL-44. The prototype appeared in 1946 as a 48.00 tonne heavy tank with thick armour and a 700hp (522kW) Maybach petrol engine. Only 60 out of a planned 300 were built, and these served between 1947 and 1953, eventually being replaced not by the proposed AMX-50 but by US medium tanks, as France began to develop its own concept of combined-arms warfare and a new type of tank.

The first French tank of post-war design to enter service was the Char AMX-13 light tank, designed at the Atelier de Construction d'Issy-les-Moulineaux (AMX), and built first by the Atelier de Construction de Roanne before construction was transferred to Creusot-Loire at Chalon-sur-Saône. The origins of the AMX-13 lay with a 1946 requirement of the French airborne forces for a tank that could provide their forces with medium fire-support: the requirement therefore demanded a high-velocity 75mm (2.95in) gun, air-portability and a maximum weight of 13.00 tonnes. This attractive combination of features appealed both to the French army, which became the major operator of the resultant type for reconnaissance and tank-destroying roles, and to a number of other armies, who appreciated the AMX-13's heavy firepower and modest cost: the cost, combined with the vehicle's simplicity and reliability, attracted armies that were in the process of establishing armoured forces for the first time.

The prototype appeared in 1948, and revealed its origins in its lightweight construction, configuration, and the use of a low-profile oscillating turret. The hull was of all-welded construction, supported on each side by five road wheels with torsion bar suspension. The hull accommodated the driver (left) and engine (right) at the front together with the transmission to the front drive sprockets; there were two or three track-return rollers on each side. The centre and rear of the hull housed the Fives-Cail Babcock FL-10

115

turret, an oscillating type whose fixed lower portion (located on the turret ring) had the trunnions that carry the oscillating upper portion together with the 75mm (2.95in) fixed gun, plus the commander (left) and gunner (right). Traverse was achieved hydraulically or manually by the complete turret, while elevation was achieved hydraulically or manually by the upper portion. This had the advantage of minimising the overall height of the vehicle, and permitted the use of an automatic loader for the main gun. The adoption of an automatic loader ensured that no tactical capability was lost in having only a three-man crew, which in turn allowed the designers to keep the tank smaller and lighter than would have been the case with a four-man crew. A variant of the AMX-13 intended for North African operations had the FL-11 turret with a manually loaded gun, and was distinguishable by its lack of a turret bustle. The next variant was fitted with the FL-12 turret carrying a 105mm (4.13in) GIAT 105/57 gun, a rifled weapon designed to fire non-rotating rounds. Most older AMX-13s in French service were revised with the 90mm (3.54in) GIAT CN90F3 gun able to fire a more advanced range of modern ammunition types, but some retained the smaller gun and in recompense gained four SS.11 wire-guided anti-tank missiles, which were replaced in the late 1960s by six more-advanced HOT anti-tank missiles.

The only other nation in the Western alliance to develop new tanks in the late 1940s and 1950s was the USA, which unlike the USSR, had ended World War II with a vast number of vehicles mostly designed in the early 1940s and which were approaching obsolescence. The USA could therefore not allow any delay in the development of new types (based mainly on the few types that entered service late in the war, but revised in the light of analysis of World War II operations and the emergence of the USSR as the main threat). The older tanks were acquired by the newly created armoured forces of American allies, allowing a new generation of armoured fighting vehicles to be adopted.

The most important of the late-World War II vehicles was the Heavy Tank M26 Pershing, which was reclassified as a medium tank in May 1946 following the final American recognition that the wartime classification of vehicles (medium tanks for the 'maid-of-all-work' roles, heavy tanks for the support role and tank destroyers for the tank-killing role) was spurious. The new medium tank classification used for the Pershing paved the way for what is now universally known as the main battle tank.

In 1947 it was decided to re-work the Pershing to a more workmanlike standard with the improved 90mm (3.54in) M3A1 gun in place of the original M3, and the 810hp (604kW) Continental AV-1790-5A petrol engine and Allison cross-drive transmission/steering in place of the original Ford GAF petrol engine with mechanical transmission and separate controlled-differential steering. In this guise the tank began to enter service in 1948 as the Medium Tank M46 Patton. The Patton was planned as an interim type pending deliveries of a new medium tank based on the T42 development model, but this model was still unavailable when the Korean War broke out in 1950, and the M26 and M46 therefore bore the brunt of operations in that war.

In 1949 the US Army decided to develop a new series of tanks to replace all World War II types and their derivatives still in service. These were placed under development as the Light Tank T41, the Medium Tank T42 and the Heavy Tank T43. The origins of the T41 were recognizable in the T37 light tank, whose design as a development model had been launched shortly after World War II. The T37 Phase I prototype with the 76.2mm (3in) M32 gun was completed in 1949, but already the T37 was involved in a development programme whose fruits were the T37 Phase II with a redesigned cast/welded turret, a new mantlet, revised ammunition stowage,

Entering service in 1951 and later named in honour of General Walker, the bulldog-like commander of the US forces in Korea at the beginning of the Korean War, the M41 was the last true light tank developed in the USA. This is still in service with a number of countries, and despite its small size offers moderately good protection, considerable performance and agility, and a 3in (76.2mm) main gun that was notably powerful at the time of the tank's adoption and is still an effective weapon for a vehicle now used mainly for the reconnaissance role.

and a fire-control system that integrated a coincidence rangefinder with a Vickers stabilizer for the gun mounting, and the T27 Phase III with an automatic loader for the main armament, and an IBM stabilizer for the gun mounting. The T37 Phase II became the starting point for the T41, which was finally standardized in 1950 as the Light Tank M41 Little Bulldog, although the name was subsequently changed to Walker Bulldog in honour of the small but pugnacious US commander in Korea. Production began in 1950, and some 5,500 M51 series vehicles were built.

In design, the M41 made full use of US combat experience in World War II, and it is in many ways similar to the M24 it was designed to replace. The all-welded hull is arranged into the standard three compartments, with the driver in the forward compartment, the commander, gunner and loader in the turret/basket assembly over the central compartment, and the 500hp (373kW)´ Continental AOS-895-3 petrol engine in the rear compartment, to power the rear drive sprockets via the cross-drive transmission. The running gear consists on each side of five road wheels with independent torsion bar suspension, and there are three track-return rollers and a front idler. The powered turret is mainly of cast construction with a welded roof and bustle, and accommodates the M32 L/52/1 unstabilized gun. Later variants of the Walker Bulldog were the M41A1, M41A2 and M41A3 which differed only in detail, including an increase in main armament stowage.

The last variants had the AOSI-895-5 engine, a fuel-injected version of the standard unit.

The M41 and its derivatives are still in moderately extensive service, current update packages centring on the powerplant and armament, for which a diesel engine and a 90mm (3.54in) weapon are offered.

The T42 medium tank did not enjoy as successful a career. It had been realized fairly early in the M26's career that the turret lacked the ballistic shaping to provide adequate protection against the best anti-tank projectiles beginning to appear in the mid-1940s, and the T42 project was designed to remedy this deficiency. However, when the Korean War started the hull of the T42 was still not ready for production, and it was decided to produce another interim type by combining the hull of the M46 with the turret of the T42, complete with its 90mm (3.54in) M36 gun, to produce the M46A1 (converted models) and the Medium Tank M47 Patton (production models). The improved turret shape further highlighted the Americans' steady progress towards the Soviet pattern of battle tank, with a more curvaceous turret located well forward in front of an extensive rear decking: the increased length of current tank guns dictated that when the tank was out of combat, the turret was generally traversed to the rear as a means of reducing the vehicle's overall length. Despite its interim nature, the M47 was produced to a total of 8,576 examples. The M36 gun was a L/43/1 development of the M1 anti-aircraft gun.

The M47 entered service in 1952, but as an interim type did not remain in service for very long. As soon as supplies of M48s began to arrive in useful numbers, the M47 was withdrawn and reallocated to the USA's allies under the Military Aid Program. The tank is still in widespread service, and in many countries has been upgraded with a diesel powerplant and improved armament, the latter sometimes including the 105mm (4.13in) M68 gun with a more modern fire-control system.

Development of the Medium Tank M48 Patton began in October 1950 at the Detroit Arsenal, and as its name suggests this is an evolutionary development of the M46 and M47. The first T48 prototype appeared in December 1951, and the type was ordered into production during the following March at two major construction facilities, some 11,700 being built before production ended in 1959. The production commitment occurred at a time when the Americans were worried that the Korean War could escalate towards a third world war, and this demanded the rapid production of new battle tanks. However, when the tank began to reach service units in 1953 it became clear that the production decision had been reached too quickly, and most of the early M48s had to be virtually rebuilt in a costly programme to eliminate the mechanical teething problems that had not been obviated by the development programme.

By comparison with the M47, the M48 introduced a cast hull and a cast turret of revised shape for a vehicle that was slightly shorter, wider and lower than its predecessor. The same engine and transmission were used, but despite an increase in combat weight compared with the M47, the M48

The value of the M41 Walker Bulldog light tank lay not in the type of high-intensity warfare envisaged for Europe, where the two superpower blocs faced each other across Germany, but in the lower-intensity warfare that flared up in areas such as South-East Asia. These M41s are seen during a 1962 training deployment to Thailand.

The M48A3 was one of the most important M48 variants as it introduced a diesel-engined powerplant for greater range in combination with the greater operational safety associated with the low-volatility fuel used by this type of engine, and was also fitted with a more advanced fire-control system than earlier M48 variants. The type had a crew of four and a combat weight of 46.4 tons, its protection was afforded by steel armour varying in thickness between a minimum of 12.7mm (0.5in) and a maximum of 120mm (4.8in), and its armament comprised a 3.54in (90mm) main gun with 62 rounds of ammunition and two machine-guns: the latter comprised one 0.3in (7.62mm) weapon co-axial with the main gun and supplied with 6,000 rounds of ammunition, and one 0.5in (12.7mm) weapon with 630 rounds of ammunition on the commander's hatch for local protection and anti-aircraft use. The type was powered by a 750hp (559kW) Continental AVDS-1790-2A diesel engine for performance that included a speed of 30mph (48km/h) and a range of 288 miles (463km). The vehicle's overall dimensions included a length of 24ft 5in (7.442m) with the main gun trained directly forward, a width of 11ft 11in (3.63m) and a height of 10ft 3in (3.12m).

was slightly faster. The baseline M48 was followed by the M48A1 with detail improvements, the M48A2 with a fuel-injected engine and a larger fuel capacity, the M48A3 (rebuilt M48A1 and M48A2) with the 750hp (559kW) AVDS-1790-2A diesel engine, and the M48A5 (rebuilt M48A1 and M48A3) with a host of improvements pioneered on other models and a 105mm (4.13in) L68 main gun. Like other battle tanks of its period, the M48 was improved with operational additions such as infra-red lights and upgraded fire-control systems, and in more recent years several manufacturers in the USA and elsewhere have offered modernization packages for an updated diesel engine, a 105mm (4.13in) gun and other advanced features.

By the mid-1950s the M48 was maturing into a powerful battle tank, but in 1956 it was decided to press ahead with the development of an M48 derivative with greater firepower, superior mobility and reliability, and enhanced range. Greater firepower and superior mobility were clearly desirable in a tank whose primary object was to tackle and defeat main battle tanks of the type epitomized by the Soviet T-54 and T-55 series with their 100mm (3.94in) L/54 guns; whilst better reliability and enhanced range offered significant battlefield advantages at all operational levels. To date, the Americans had been relatively unconcerned by deficiencies in range and reliability: in World War II they had deployed so large a logistical back-up capability that any such shortfalls in their tanks did not seriously affect the tempo of operations. But by the mid-1950s, the changing nature of warfare persuaded the Americans that greater unrefuelled range (and greater reliability) were required, as these logistical services could no longer be guaranteed to front-line forces in the type of fluid warfare that seemed inevitable.

The hull and running gear of the M48 were deemed more than adequate as the basis of the new tank, which was thus an evolutionary development rather than a completely new design. In November 1956, an M48 hull was

re-engined with the AVDS-1790-P diesel engine, and extensive tests yielded highly successful results. In February 1958 the concept was taken a step further when three M48A2s were re-engined with the diesel powerplant as the prototypes for the XM60 series, and these were also successfully tested under a range of operational, climatic and geographical conditions.

The final part of the improvement package over the M48 rested with the new tank's firepower, which had to be markedly superior to that of the 90mm (3.54in) M41 L/48 gun of the M48 series, and in October and November 1958 a number of candidate weapons were trialled before the decision was made in favour of the 105mm (4.13in) M68, which combined the barrel of the British L7 with an American breech. Work had been developing on the refinement of the complete package, and the selection of the main armament allowed the Main Battle Tank M60 to be standardized in March 1959, with the initial production contract let to the Chrysler Corporation in June 1959 for 180 examples to be built at the Delaware Defense Plant. Production later switched to the Detroit Tank Plant, which then became the USA's only major tank production facility. Production continued into mid-1985, when the M60 production line was closed after the delivery of more than 15,000 vehicles for the US and export markets.

The M60 entered service with the US Army in 1960, and in numerical terms remained the most important US tank until it was supplemented and then largely supplanted in first-line units by the M1 Abrams during the 1980s and 1990s. The initial M60 variant weighed 46.27 tonnes and was powered by a 750hp (559kW) AVDS-1790-2A diesel engine. The M60 can be regarded only as an interim model, for it retained the basic turret of the M48 that was recognized as failing to provide adequate levels of ballistic protection. In October 1962, therefore, the M60 was replaced in production by the M60A1 with the new 'needle-nosed' turret that offered both superior ballistic protection and greater internal volume. This helped to increase the main armament's ammunition stowage and improve its elevation arc. The modified turret also altered the ammunition capacities for the 7.62mm (0.3in) co-axial and 0.5in (12.7mm) anti-aircraft machine-guns, the latter located on a trim commander's cupola. The overall weight of the M60A1 is 48.99 tonnes,

The US Army's current mainstay battle tank is the M1 Abrams with a gas turbine powerplant and a large measure of composite armour. The type is used in four main variants, namely the basic M1 (illustrated) with a 4.13in (105mm) rifled main gun, the M1A1 with a 4.72in (120mm) smooth-bore main gun, the M1A2 with an automatic loader allowing the reduction of the crew from four to three, and the M1A3 development of the M1A2 with a number of protection and mobility enhancements.

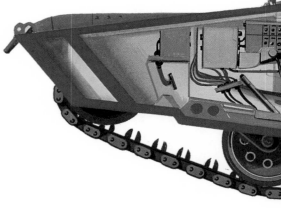

but the engine and performance remain unaltered despite a fractional reduction in fuel capacity.

The M60A1 was the initial definitive production model, and was made of large castings welded together to create the hull and turret. There is no stabilization system for the gun in either elevation or azimuth, but the necessities of modern war are reflected in the provision of night-vision equipment and, most importantly of all, a central filtration system that supplies air cleaned of NBC (nuclear, biological and chemical) warfare agents to the four crew members via individual tubes. And the requirements of independent operations are further reflected in provision of dozer blade attachments for the preparation of fire positions; in addition, the M60A1 possesses deep-wading capability.

The M60 was still at a comparatively early stage of its career (which has seen development well into the 1990s), but as its basic design lies with the philosophies of the 1950s, the tank's complete history is described here.

Whilst the M68 gun was being developed and accepted, the US Army was considering alternative anti-tank weapons for future armoured fighting vehicles, and decided that a better method of defeating modern armour might lie with the guided missile; this resulted in development by Philco-Ford of the MGM-51 Shillelagh tube-launched missile for use by the M551 Sheridan (often called a light tank although the US Army rightly designates it a reconnaissance vehicle). The missile was designed to be fired from a 152mm (6in) gun/launcher, and after leaving the gun/launcher deployed its control surfaces for guidance by an infra-red system that required the gunner merely to keep the crosshairs of his sight centred on the target until the missile impacted and the HEAT warhead detonated. Considerable development problems were encountered with the missile and also with the ammunition designed for use with the same gun/launcher.

It was decided to instal the same gun/launcher in an M60 variant, with 13 missiles and 33 conventional rounds of ammunition. This M60A2 variant

This cutaway illustration highlights the internal arrangement of the M1 Abrams battle tank with the gas turbine powerplant in the rear of the hull, and the ammunition supply for the main gun in the turret bustle behind fire- and flash-proof doors with blow-out panels in its upper surface so that the force of any ammunition explosion is vented upwards rather than forward into the fighting compartment. Less readily apparent are the relatively angular external appearance, resulting from the use of composite armour that currently can only be produced in flat panels, and the advanced main gun system. This system is based on a turret that can be stabilised in azimuth and a gun that can be stabilised in elevation to allow accurate fire with the tank on the move across country, and on an advanced fire-control system with a digital computer to generate high-quality solutions to any fire-control problem on the basis of data provided by stabilised day and night optical and thermal sensors, a laser ranger, sensors for ambient conditions (external temperature, air pressure, and wind speed and direction, and internal factors such as ammunition temperature) and standardised data for the various ammunition parameters.

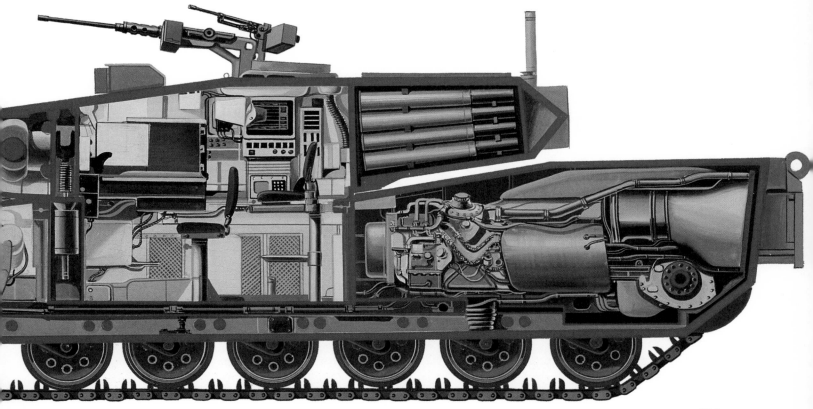

Most modern tanks, typified here by an M60, can be fitted with extra equipment such as a dozer blade for the creation of semi-concealed fire positions, with only the turret protruding above ground level, and for tasks such as the creation of ramps facilitating entry and exit to obstacles such as river banks.

was developed in 1964 and 1965 for its production debut in 1966: some indication of the gun/launcher and ammunition/missile development problems can be gained from the facts that the first M60A2 unit became operational only in 1972, and that total M60A2 production was a mere 526 vehicles, which were withdrawn after only a short first-line career for conversion as required into specialized derivatives of the M60 series, such as the M60 Armored Vehicle-Launched Bridge and M728 Combat Engineer Vehicle.

Service experience with the M60 and M60A1 had meanwhile suggested a variety of ways in which the basic tank could be upgraded mechanically, and a number of retrofit packages were developed. The most significant of these are the so-called RISE (Reliability Improved Selected Equipment) modification of the engine, two-axis stabilization for the main armament, an upgraded fire-control system, and improved night-vision equipment. These and other modifications are the hallmarks of the final variant, the M60A3, that is in essence a product-improved M60A1 that began to enter production in February 1978. New-production examples are complemented in service by M60A1 machines retrofitted to virtually the same standard with items such as a thermal sleeve to reduce main

The Pz 61 was the first battle tank of Swiss design, and was an unexceptional but very well made vehicle with an unstabilised 4.13in (105mm) main gun. Production of 150 such tanks was completed between 1964 and 1968.

armament barrel distortion caused by differential heating, a top-loading air cleaner, and passive night-vision devices.

The M60A3 incorporates all these features, as well as British-type smoke-dischargers on each side of the turret, an engine smoke generator, an automatic engine fire-extinguishing system, and a much improved fire-control system. This last system was developed by Hughes with a laser rather than optical rangefinder and a solid-state digital rather than mechanical analog computer. Like that of British tanks, the M60's success rests mainly with its good protection and firepower, although some reservations have been expressed about mobility and the M60's high silhouette, a factor exacerbated by the commander's substantial cupola.

The heavyweight companion to the M41 light and M60 medium (now main battle) tanks was the Heavy Tank M103, of which only 200 were produced. The cast hull was basically that of the M48 lengthened by the addition of an extra track-return roller and two road wheels on each side, and the turret was a very large cast unit that accommodated a crew of four (commander located immediately behind the gun, gunner and two loaders) and the massive 120mm (4.72in) M58 L/60gun. The vehicle was fitted with the powerplant and transmission of the M47 battle tank, and at a weight of 56.70 tonnes was underpowered to a serious degree and so lacked mobility. It was 1957 before the type was finally cleared for service as the M103A1, which was soon replaced by the M60. The other main operator of the type was the US Marine Corps, which used 156 M103A2 tanks produced by converting surplus M103A1s with AVDS-1790-2AD diesel engines.

The only other Western nation to develop an indigenous tank in the 1950s was Switzerland, a country with a long record of tank operation, although until the development of the first Swiss tank in the 1950s these had all been imported or licence-built machines. The Swiss programme resulted in the kW 30 prototype that appeared in 1958 with a Swiss-designed 90mm (3.54in) main gun and Belleville washer suspension for its arrangement of six road wheels on each side. The kW 30 was joined by a similar prototype in 1959, and later by 10 examples of the Pz 58 pre-production version with the British 20pdr (83.4mm/3.28in) gun. The pace of tank development in this period was unrelenting, and the Pz 61 production model that entered service in 1965 mounted a British 105mm (4.13in) L7 gun. This model had a cast hull and turret, each an impressive single-piece casting, weighed 38.00 tonnes and was powered by a 630hp (470kW) MTU MB 837 diesel engine.

After 150 Pz 61s the production line switched to the improved Pz 68, which

The Pz 68 was an improved and generally updated version of the Pz 61, and 170 examples of this battle tank were delivered to the Swiss army in the period between 1971 and 1973, with features such as an uprated engine, an improved fire-control system and a main gun stabilised in azimuth and elevation.

first appeared in 1968 and was then built to the extent of 170 tanks. This model is similar to the Pz 61 in all essential details but for the addition of a two-axis stabilization system for the main gun, and a 650hp (485kW) MB 837 diesel powerplant for superior performance at a weight of 39.70 tonnes. Gun-armed variants of this initial model, which was redesignated the Pz 68 Mk 1 when the later variants appeared, are the Pz 68 Mk 2 with a thermal sleeve for the main armament (50 built), the Pz 58 Mk 3 based on the Mk 2 but with a larger turret (110 built), and the Pz 68 Mk 4 based on the Mk 3 (60 built).

On the other side of the Iron Curtain all tank development was concentrated in Soviet hands, and pressed ahead feverishly on the basis of late-World War II developments. The two most important types in Soviet service at the end of World War II were the T-34/85 medium tank and IS-3 heavy tank, which were deemed adequate for first-line service through the remainder of the 1940s. But the Soviets were not content to rest on their laurels, and a classic new tank was developed from the T-44 medium tank (that was built in small numbers during 1945 and 1946 but proved mechanically unreliable). This was the Main Battle Tank T-54, which appeared in prototype form during 1946 and entered production at Kharkov in 1947 for service in 1949 or 1950. The T-54 and its Main Battle Tank T-55 derivative were built in larger numbers than any other tank in the period after World War II, and it is estimated that before production ceased in 1981, more than 50,000 examples had come off the main production lines in Kharkov and Omsk in the USSR, and off other lines in China (as the Type 59), Czechoslovakia and Poland.

The driver is seated in a forward compartment on the left, and there is a fixed 7.62mm (0.3in) machine-gun for use by the driver. To the driver's right, instead of the bow machine-gun and its gunner of earlier tanks, are

The M113 series of tracked armoured personnel carriers is the most important of its type anywhere in the Western world, and is an amphibious type of largely aluminium construction. This American basic vehicle has been used as the core of a host of important armed and unarmed variants.

main armament ammunition stowage, the vehicle's batteries and a modest quantity of fuel. At the rear of the vehicle is the compartment for the 520hp (388kW) V-54 diesel engine and transmission. This overall arrangement leaves the centre of the vehicle for the fighting compartment, whose elegantly shaped turret had a manual traverse system in early models, revised to an electro-hydraulic system with manual back-up in later models. The turret is a single casting with a welded two-piece roof and a rotating floor rather than a turret basket, and accommodates the commander, gunner and loader together with the 100mm (3.94in) D-10T gun in somewhat cramped conditions. This is still a useful weapon, but in the T-54 is now let down by its simple fire-control system, which relies on optical sighting by the commander and gunner. This was considered adequate when the T-54 was introduced, but increasingly became a limiting feature as the type remained in service. The other main limitations suffered by T-54 crews include the small main armament ammunition stowage of 34 rounds, the use of external (and highly vulnerable) fuel tanks to boost range, and the poor elevation arc of the main gun, which makes it all but impossible for the T-54 to adopt a hull-down tactical position, and this places great emphasis on the good ballistic protection provided by the tank's shaping.

Given the longevity of its production and service careers, the T-54 has inevitably undergone a number of modifications and improvements, including an NBC system on later models (also retrofitted to earlier models). Most T-54s were later fitted with infra-red driving equipment and received the revised designation T-54(M). First seen in the mid-1950s, the T-54A has improved main armament in the form of the D-10TG gun with a bore evacuator, stabilization in the vertical plane and powered elevation; when retrofitted with infra-red driving lights it is designated the T-54A(M). In 1957 the Soviets introduced the T-54B and, apart from being the first model produced with infra-red night-vision devices as standard, it has the D-10T2S main gun with two-axis stabilization. Variously described as the T-54C or T-54X, the next model is identical with the T-54B except that the gunner's cupola is replaced by a plain forward-opening hatch.

These collective modifications resulted in a basically similar tank with the revised designation Main Battle Tank T-55, which was introduced in the late 1950s with standard features such as no loader's cupola with its 12.7mm (0.5in) anti-aircraft machine-gun, no turret dome ventilator, and a 580hp (432kW) V-55 diesel engine of 500km (311 miles) range rather than 400km (249 miles); the 12.7mm (0.5in) machine-gun was reinstated on some tanks which were then designated T-55(M). Seen for the first time in 1963, the T-55A is the final production version, and is similar to the T-55 apart from having a 7.62mm (0.3in) PKT co-axial machine-gun in place of the original SGMT of the same calibre, an increase in main armament ammunition stowage due to removal of the bow machine-gun, and a number of detail improvements such as an anti-radiation lining; when fitted with the 12.7mm (0.5in) anti-aircraft machine-gun this model is designated the T-55A(M).

The T-54 and T-55 are no longer in service with the former-Soviet forces, but are widely used by many of the former-USSR's clients and allies, who have often carried out their own modification and update programmes. The most important of these have included replacement of the Soviet 100mm (3.94in) main gun with a British or American 105mm (4.13in) weapon. Despite its tactical failings by comparison with the latest Western tanks, the T-54 and T-55 remain important weapons and the very simplicity that makes them obsolescent against the West is an invaluable asset in countries with limited mechanical resources and trained manpower. In general, the T-54 and T-55 can be equated with the American M60A1.

The Soviets' best heavy tank at the end of World War II was the IS-3.

Advent of the Mechanised Infantry Fighting Vehicle

ONE of the most important lessons of World War II was that armoured formations could generally move faster than their companion infantry formations, even when the latter were of the motorised type carried in trucks until they approached the scene of action and disembarked to fight as standard infantry, and that tanks without infantry support were relatively easy targets for the enemy's artillery.

This led to the creation of the first truly mechanised formations that combined tank and infantry units in tracked or, in the case of the infantry unit, half-tracked vehicles that provided the embarked troops with protection against small-arms fire and shell fragments and could match their tank brethren in basic cross-country mobility.

The most important vehicle for this infantry task in World War II was the half-track carrier epitomised by the American M2 and M3 vehicles, although small-scale use was also made of obsolete tanks stripped of their turrets so that the fighting compartment could be used for the accommodation of a small number of infantrymen. So successful were these first attempts that after World War II considerable attention was paid to the creation of specialised armoured personnel carriers (APCs) based on multi-wheeled or, wherever possible, fully tracked chassis. Although some of the early APCs had open-topped accommodation, it was soon realised that overhead protection was vital, and in its fully fledged form the APC soon became a box-like tracked vehicle with a rear compartment for the carriage of infantry, who could disembark with considerable speed through a large door or, in vehicles such as the M113, a rear wall that was designed to hinge down to create a large ramp.

It was not long before these APCs began to be seen as more than mere infantry transports, and a trainable machine-gun was therefore provided for the vehicle commander, who could therefore provide covering fire for the troops as they disembarked, and could also provide a measure of self-protection against the attentions of enemy infantry. Further expansion of this concept led to the mechanized infantry fighting vehicle (MCV) such as the German Marder, with a turreted cannon for genuine if limited offensive capability against other light armoured fightinf vehicles, trucks and other 'soft' targets.

Immediately after the end of the war the Soviet army began to receive the improved IS-4 with the same 122mm (4.8in) main gun. This was the starting point for IS-5, IS-6, IS-7, IS-8 and IS-9 prototypes in the late 1940s and early 1950s. Stalin died in 1953, and when the IS-9 was placed in production during 1956 the letter prefix was altered to 'T', so that the service version of the IS-9 became the T-10, which began to reach operational units in 1957. Production amounted to some 2,500 such tanks in the late 1950s, and its role was heavy support for the T-54 and T-55. The hull was of the same rolled armour construction as the IS-3, but was lengthened by the addition of a seventh road wheel on each side. The main armament was an improved version of the IS-3's 122mm (4.8in) D-25 L/43 gun, in this instance designated D-74. The other armament was a pair of 12.7mm (0.5in) machine-guns, one located co-axially and the other on the turret roof as an anti-aircraft weapon.

The 49.80 tonne T-10 was succeeded by the more capable T-10M with 14.5mm (0.57in) rather than 12.7mm (0.5in) machine-guns, a multi-baffle rather than double-baffle muzzle brake on the main armament, two-axis stabilization for the main armament, enhanced night-vision capability, and an NBC system. The revised T-10M weighed 46.25 tonnes, and maintained the T-10's striking resemblance to the IS-3, although its armour was revised and thickened, while the use of a 690hp (515kW) V-2-IS (otherwise V-2K) diesel engine provided for a higher maximum speed.

The M551 Sheridan remains something of an oddity, for it was basically a light tank fitted with a 5.98in (152mm) main 'gun' designed either to fire a low-velocity anti-tank projectile or serve as the launch tube for the MGM-51 Shillelagh anti-tank missile, which used an infra-red link for command to line of sight guidance. The missile was never completely satisfactory, but the M551 was retained in American service as it is easily air-portable and therefore well suited to the requirement of the US airborne forces, which operate the type in the reconnaissance role.

This inside view of the M551 Sheridan's turret reveals the relative complexity of a type designed in the late 1950s and early 1960s.

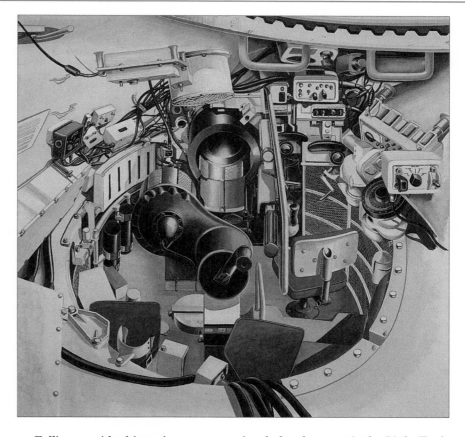

Falling outside this main sequence of tank development is the Light Tank PT-76, which appeared in service during 1952 as evidence of the Soviets' return to the concept of a light amphibious vehicle for deep reconnaissance. Developed from a lightweight cross-country vehicle and Soviet light tanks of the late World War II period, the PT-76 has the advantages of simplicity and moderate offensive capability; this has made the type popular with former-Soviet client states requiring a machine matched to their poor communications and lack of a large industrialized base for the support and maintenance of more advanced tanks. The main failings of the PT-76 and other amphibious light tanks include their large size to provide adequate volume for buoyancy, thin armour which leaves the PT-76 vulnerable even to heavy machine-gun fire, and the sacrifice to weight-saving of features such as an NBC system and night-vision equipment. The welded hull of the 14.00 tonne PT-76 accommodates the driver in a forward compartment, the fighting compartment in the centre and the engine compartment at the rear. The 240hp (179kW) V-6 diesel engine is essentially half of the V-2 used in the T-54/T-55 series, and provides maximum land and water speeds of 44km/h and 10km/h (27.3mph and 6.2mph) respectively. The electrically/manually-powered turret is of welded steel, and accommodates the commander, who doubles as gunner, and the loader for the 76.2mm (3in) D-56T gun, which is a development of the weapon used in the T-34 and KV-1 tanks of World War II.

The PT-76 has appeared in a number of forms as the PT-76 Model 1 with a multiple-slotted muzzle brake, the PT-76 Model 2 with a double-baffle muzzle brake and a bore evacuator, the PT-76 Model 3 similar to the Model 2 but without a bore evacuator, and the PT-76 Model 4 (or PT-76B) with the D-56TM gun with two-axis stabilization. The PT-76 is still in very widespread service, and is likely to remain so for the foreseeable future due to the lack of an adequate replacement.

Modern Tanks

THE tanks of the 1950s may be characterized as logical developments of the best features to emerge from World War II: new features did appear, but in almost every instance these were grafted onto tanks that could have (and indeed often had) been developed in that war. Tanks were used extensively in the period up to 1960, especially by the Soviets in dealing with revolts and revolutions by their eastern European subjects, but true armoured warfare had been rare. The Korean War (1950-53) saw considerable use of tanks by the United Nations' forces, although mainly in the support rather than anti-tank role, and the most significant episodes of tank warfare in the period were the Arab-Israeli wars of 1947-48 and 1956. In these wars the Israelis secured major victories over larger and theoretically more powerful foes through the adventurous use of high-quality armoured forces in deep outflanking and penetration movements, destroying the Arab forces' cohesion and lines of communication. These were essentially the tactics of World War II with their pace quickened by ideal tank terrain, and confirmed the continued dominance of the tank under conditions of air superiority.

By 1960, however, a new generation of tanks had begun to emerge, which, whilst building on previous experience and practice, were notable for their adoption of the best of modern features that had been retrofitted into the tanks of the 1950s. Combined with these technical features (gun stabilization systems, computer-aided fire-control systems, night-vision equipment, NBC protection, and advanced ammunition) were improvements in protection, mobility and firepower. Armour continued to increase in thickness, and was also better conceived and designed for superior protection against the diversity of modern ammunition types, increasingly complemented by surface- and air-launched guided missiles. Mobility was enhanced by the adoption of increasingly powerful yet compact engines to improve power-to-weight ratios. And firepower was enhanced by the adoption of larger-calibre main guns, firing improved projectiles with the aid of increasingly sophisticated fire-control systems to create a significantly higher first-round hit probability. Typical of the improved projectiles are the comparatively

The Hagglund Ikv 91 is a relatively rare creature for a modern army, being a dedicated tank destroyer based on the Pbv 302 armoured personnel carrier chassis and hull with a revolving turret carrying a 3.54in (90mm) high-velocity gun.

Being relatively lightly protected and indifferently armed, the M551 Sheridan is best suited to the reconnaissance role in areas where it can exploit its performance and agility to avoid engagement by more powerfully armed opponents.

slow-moving HEAT warhead designed to generate an armour-piercing jet of super-hot gas and molten metal that can burn its way through protective armour, and the extremely fast-moving APFSDS designed as a fin-stabilized dart of heavy metal (normally tungsten or depleted uranium) that discards its supporting sabots on leaving the gun barrel, and delivers a devastating kinetic blow to the armour.

During the early 1950s the main tanks in service with the British forces were the Centurion medium and Conqueror heavy types. These were recognized as among the best vehicles in their classes, but it was also appreciated that Soviet developments would soon redress the USSR's qualitative inferiority, and the search was initiated for a single type to supersede both the Centurion and Conqueror, offering the mobility of the former with the firepower of the latter, but in a modern package. Various experimental designs were drawn up, but none of these progressed past the drawing board stage until Leyland produced two examples of its FV4202. This was perceived as a research rather than a pre-production design, but it pioneered two of the key features later adopted for the Chieftain: a turret without a gun mantlet, and a semi-reclined driver position, allowing considerable reduction in hull height.

The same reconnaissance task is performed for the British army by the Scorpion, otherwise known as the Combat Vehicle Reconnaissance (Tracked). The Scorpion is fast and nippy, and its 3in (76.2mm) main gun is a low-pressure type designed to fire the effective HESH round.

The Vickers Main Battle Tank is something of a rarity by modern standards for it was designed as a private venture, in this instance to meet a requirement issued by the Indian army for a battle tank that could be made under licence in India and maintained by unsophisticated troops, yet still offer a good account of itself on the modern battlefield. In its Mk I form the Vickers Main Battle Tank was sold to India and Kuwait, and in its Mk 3 form (illustrated) with a diesel rather than a petrol powerplant was delivered to Kenya and Nigeria.

When it was re-created in 1956, the West German army was equipped mostly with US weapons, including the M47 and M48A2 tanks: the M47 was already in widespread service, and was thus cheap, and presented even an inexperienced service with no problems, while the smaller number of M48A2s offered superior combat capabilities to crews who had mastered the M47. From the beginning, however, the West German army realized that its tactical concepts, inherited from its vast experience of European armoured warfare in World War II, were at variance with US concepts, which stressed firepower and protection to the detriment of agility and the battlefield advantages of modest weight and low overall silhouette. The US main battle tanks of the period turned the scales at about 50.80 tonnes, but the West German army thought that a figure nearer 30.00 tonnes should be the norm for operations in Western Europe. In 1957, therefore, the West German army called for a new tank weighing a maximum of 30.00 tonnes, powered by an air-cooled multi-fuel engine for a minimum power-to-weight ratio of 22kW/tonne (30hp/ton).

France and Italy had reached much the same conclusions as the West Germans, and France and West Germany were able to sign an interim

Developed by Thyssen Henschel in Germany, on the basis of the TAM medium battle tank it had designed for Argentina and using the chassis, hull and automotive system of the Marder mechanised infantry combat vehicle, the TH 301 was an improved prototype that failed to secure any production order.

The Chieftain battle tank was the mainstay of the British armoured force between the Centurion and the current Challenger, and in keeping with the British philosophy of armoured warfare offered excellent firepower and protection at the expense of performance and agility.

understanding about the development of the new vehicle. Thus two prototypes were produced in France by AMX, and two different prototypes by each of two West German consortia: Gruppe A led by Porsche and Gruppe B by Ruhrstahl. A turret to suit all these prototypes was ordered from Rheinmetall. The two Gruppe A vehicles were delivered in January 1961 and the two Gruppe B machines in September of the same year. Given the nature of the specification, it was hardly surprising that the two vehicle types were similar in overall line, and were powered by the same Daimler-Benz MB 838 multi-fuel engine.

The Challenger is an altogether more formidable machine: an evolutionary development of the Chieftain with all the advantages that accrue from such a practice in terms of low technical risk, reduced development cost and contracted development time. The Challenger entered service in 1983 and is essentially the Shir 2 revised to accord with British operational requirements, and fitted with the Chobham composite armour first trialled during 1971 on a Chieftain derivative, the FV4211 prototype. Although based on the Chieftain in its structure and layout, the Challenger has a different appearance through the use of the special Chobham laminate armour, which comprises layers of special ceramics, metal and other material to provide a very high level of impenetrability to anti-armour weapons of both the chemical and kinetic varieties. To date, Chobham armour can be produced only in flat sheets, and this means that

The Chieftain was designed for service in the type of landscape seen here, namely the relatively close country of West Germany where any Soviet invasion of Western Europe was expected to materialise between the late 1950s and late 1980s. Optimisation for this type of battlefield meant that the Chieftain was well gunned and heavily armoured, but not notable for its performance.

specially shaped panels have to be laid over a steel inner structure to produce hull and turret contours less curvaceous than those of the Chieftain. The Challenger also has the Condor 12V 1200 diesel engine and an automatic transmission in an easily removed powerpack, revised suspension for a better cross-country ride, the TOGS sight and the IFCS fire-control system. The armament is currently the L11A5 gun, although the production version of the XL30 high-pressure gun is planned for retrofit as soon as possible.

Introduced in 1965, the Leopard 1 is in marked contrast to the Chieftain: whereas the priority list for the British tank was firepower, protection and mobility, that for the West German tank was firepower and mobility (as equal first) and then protection. Since 1965 the Leopard 1 has proved eminently successful, the total of 2,437 vehicles built for the West German army being complemented by export sales to Australia (90 vehicles), Belgium (334 vehicles), Canada (114), Denmark (120), Greece (106), Italy (920), the Netherlands (468), Norway (78) and Turkey (77).

Like the Chieftain, the Leopard 1 is of conventional layout but with only two compartments: that for the crew of four (the driver in the hull, and the commander, gunner and loader in the turret) at the front, and that for the powerpack at the rear. The manual transmission drives rear sprockets, and the running gear comprises, on each side, seven dual road wheels with independent torsion bar suspension and four track-return rollers. And as with the Chieftain, the Leopard 1 has night-vision devices, smoke-dischargers on each side of the turret (triple units), an overpressure NBC system, and metal-reinforced rubber skirts. The armament is a British-supplied 105mm (4.13in) L7A3 weapon firing the standard range of NATO ammunition, of which 55 rounds were carried; but when first delivered, the Leopard 1 lacked any gun stabilization and a sophisticated fire-control system.

Given that low weight was important to the Leopard 1, armour of only modest thickness was inevitable. The Leopard 1 has much in common with the German battle tanks of World War II, being fairly angular in shape and possessing sharply angled armour only on the hull front and upper sides. The hull is of welded construction, while the turret is a cast unit.

Just as the Chieftain paved the way for the Challenger in British service,

the Leopard 1 paved the way for the Leopard 2 in West German service. This resulted from the cancellation of the planned MBT-70 collaborative tank design, and the West Germans decided to develop a new main battle tank using MBT-70 components wherever possible: the most significant of these were the MTU MB 873 multi-fuel engine and the Renk transmission. Improved Leopard 1 components had also been developed, and wherever possible these were also worked into the design of the Krauss-Maffei Leopard 2, which may be compared favourably to the T-34 as being the only tank of its period to combine firepower, protection and mobility in equal proportions. The Leopard 2's main European rivals are the Chieftain and AMX-30. The Chieftain, as discussed above, has good firepower, good protection and poor mobility, while the AMX-30, as discussed below, has good mobility, adequate firepower and poor protection.

The 1960s were years of considerable development in the armoured field, and other main battle tanks to emerge from European manufacturers were the French AMX-30 and the Swedish Strv 103. The design of the AMX-30 was carried out by AMX, while production was entrusted to the Atelier de Construction de Roanne, which completed the first production tanks in 1966 to allow a service debut in the following year. The AMX-30 is a comparatively simple tank with a hull of welded rolled armour and a cast turret, and is the lightest main battle tank of its generation. Combined with a moderately powerful engine, this produces an impressive power-to-weight ratio and thus high performance and great agility, which are both features admired by the French armoured force. Such sprightliness is bought at the expense of protection, however, and the AMX-30 must now be judged obsolescent against the heavier modern weapons, especially in flank and overhead attacks. This tendency is exacerbated by the machine's comparatively tall silhouette, created by the considerable height of the commander's cupola and its 7.62mm (0.3in) anti-aircraft machine-gun on top of an otherwise admirably low hull and turret.

The main gun is the 105mm (4.13in) GIAT CN105F1 rifled ordnance, and the AMX-30 possesses an unusual secondary armament, for although the co-axial weapon was the standard 0.5 in (12.7mm) heavy machine-gun when the AMX-30 began to enter service, this was soon replaced by a 20mm GIAT

The first battle tank designed in Germany after World War II was the Leopard, which became the Leopard I after the introduction of the considerably superior Leopard II. The type is illustrated here by the Leopard armoured recovery vehicle, which is a turretless development fitted with front-mounted dozer blade, a winch, and a small crane, which was designed especially for tasks such as the changing of a Leopard I powerpack in the field.

M693 cannon to provide a potent capability against lightly armoured targets and helicopters. The AMX-30 lacks gun stabilization and an advanced fire-control system, but has standard features such as an NBC system and night-vision equipment. This results in a tank that is somewhat cheaper to buy and easier to maintain than equivalent American, British and West German main battle tanks, with consequent advantages in the export market to less developed countries: apart from France, AMX-30 operators include Chile, Cyprus, Greece, Iraq, Qatar, Saudi Arabia, Spain, the United Arab Emirates and Venezuela.

The series is still in production, the current variant being the upgraded AMX-30 B2 with improved transmission, a COTAC integrated fire-control system (with a laser rangefinder, low-light-level TV and lead-generating computer) and other operational enhancements such as skirts, and appliqué armour for the turret.

Another main battle tank in large-scale Western service is the Americans' most important weapon of this type, the M1 Abrams. This vehicle marks a turning point in main battle tank design as it is the world's first such machine to use a gas turbine as its sole automotive engine. The origins of the type lie with West Germany's 1970 decision to pull out of the Germano-American MBT-70 programme and to concentrate instead on an indigenous tank (the Leopard 2). This left the Americans with the need to develop an M60-series successor as rapidly as possible.

In basic layout the Abrams is completely conventional, but in structure the tank reflects recent advances in protection: the Abrams is constructed of the same type of composite armour as the Challenger and Leopard 2, which explains the angularity of the tank's external contours which are conditioned by the inflexibility of the protective material added over the core structure. The driver is located in the centre of the vehicle's forward compartment, and is seated in a semi-reclining position so that the hull front can be kept low and well angled against head-on fire. Behind the driver's position is the turret, which has electro-hydraulic traverse with manual

The OTO Melara/Fiat OF-40 is an Italian battle tank designed for the export market, and makes extensive use of components and assemblies from the Leopard I, which the companies built under licence in Italy.

controls for emergency use. The main armament is the 105mm (4.13in) M68 rifled gun, which is stabilized in two axes and has power elevation; the commander and gunner are located to the right of the weapon, and the loader to its left. The fire-control system includes a Computing Devices of Canada high-speed solid-state digital computer, a Hughes Aircraft Company laser rangefinder, stabilized day/night sight and automatic sensors for static cant and wind direction/speed.

Under the raised rear decking typical of most modern battle tanks is the unusual engine, a 1,500shp (1,118ekW) Lycoming AGT-1500 gas turbine. The power delivered to the rear drive sprockets by the gas turbine is greater than that from a similarly rated diesel engine because of the gas turbine's reduced cooling requirement; this, together with its compact size and supposedly high levels of reliability, was one of the reasons for this engine type's selection. The greater power of the gas turbine gives the M1 far livelier performance than the M60A3, however, and another advantage is the fact that the engine can be run on diesel oil or kerosene (or in an emergency on petrol); the fuel tanks are separated from the crew compartment by an armoured bulkhead for increased safety. On the debit side are the engine's comparative lack of ruggedness, its high thermal signature which makes the M1 more vulnerable to heat-seeking missiles, and a specific fuel consumption high enough to offset the additional fuel capacity made possible by the smaller engine.

The last 894 M1s were completed to the Improved M1 Abrams standard with enhanced protection. Production then switched to the definitive M1A1 Abrams, which began to enter service in August 1985. This has the enhanced protection of the Improved M1, a number of detail improvements, three rather than two blow-off panels in the turret roof, integral engine smoke generators, an integrated NBC system that provides the standard conditioned breathing air and also heating or cooling for those occasions when the crew are using NBC suits and face masks. The most important modification, however, is the use of the 120mm (4.72in) Rheinmetall Rh-120

Developed as a private venture by Vickers in the UK (turret, armament and fire-control system) and FMC in the USA (chassis, automotive system and hull), the VFM 5 is an interesting attempt to combine features of two tank types, namely the armament and protection of a main battle tank with the overall weight and dimensions of a light tank.

Such was the versatility and mechanical reliability of the AMX-13 light tank that its lower hull and automotive system were used as the basis for a number of other armoured fighting vehicles such as a self-propelled gun, self-propelled anti-aircraft mounting, armoured personnel carrier, command vehicle, mortar vehicle, combat engineer vehicle and, as seen here, prototype mechanised infantry combat vehicle with a remotely controlled 20mm cannon over the rear of the hull.

smooth-bore gun in place of the original 105mm (4.13in) M68 rifled weapon for greater offensive capability and longer range. The gun mounting was designed with this change in view, so the disruption to production caused by the armament change was minimal. The considerably larger ammunition of the 120mm (4.72in) gun made a reduction in ammunition capacities inevitable: in the M1 stowage is provided for 55 rounds (44 in left- and right-hand bustle compartments each surmounted by a blow-off panel, eight in a hull compartment and three in spallproof boxes on the turret basket) while in the M1A1 there is provision for only 40 rounds (36 in left-hand, central and right-hand bustle compartments each surmounted by a blow-off panel, and four in a rear hull box).

Enhancement of the M1A1 has continued at a steady pace. M1A1 Block II vehicles have a number of detail improvements as well as an improved commander's position with an independent thermal viewer, and the M1A1 Block III is a General Dynamics proposal with a three-man crew made possible by the addition of an automatic loading system, rapid refuelling and re-ammunitioning capabilities, and improved suspension. The Abrams has suffered its fair share of problems in service, but in its M1A1 form it is certainly one of the best tanks in the world today, with a large measure of development capacity still ahead of it

Within the Soviet bloc during the 1960s and 1970s, design and construction of heavy armour was retained exclusively by the USSR, which in the late 1950s had begun to plan a successor to the T-55 and T-55 series, with the same levels of protection and mobility, but with increased firepower in the form of a 115mm (4.53in) U-5TS (or 2A20) smooth-bore gun fitted with a fume extractor and two-axis stabilization: an unusual feature of this gun is its integral spent case ejection system, activated by the gun's recoil. This is a useful feature, but had to be bought by a limitation in fire rate to only four rounds per minute with the tank stationary, as the gun has to be brought to an exact elevation for the ejection system to function. Turret

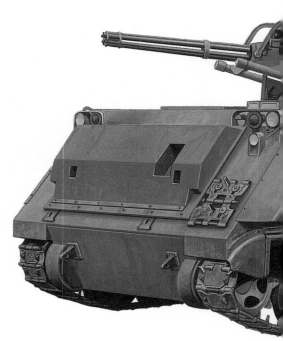

Otherwise known as the S-tank, the Strv 103 was a highly ambitious and largely successful Swedish attempt to create a small and manoeuvrable battle tank without a turret. The 4.13in (105mm) main gun is fitted with an automatic loader and is fixed in the front of the vehicle: the weapon is brought to bear by slewing the complete vehicle, whose suspension is then adjusted to secure the desired elevation angle.

The M163 is a simple and moderately effective air-defence vehicle for the short-range protection of mobile forces, and is basically an M113 armoured personnel carrier with a 20mm Vulcan six-barrel rotary cannon on a traversing and elevating mounting above it.

risks are reduced by the carriage of only four ready-use rounds in the turret, the balance of 36 rounds being carried below the turret ring (16 to the right of the driver and 20 in the rear of the fighting compartment).

The cast turret resembles that of the T-54 and T-55 series, but the welded hull is both longer and wider than that of the earlier series, with a different spacing of the road wheels. In other essential respects the T-62 is very similar to the T-55 it succeeded, and began to enter production during 1961 for service in 1963. The construction programme in the USSR lasted until 1975 and accounted for about 20,000 tanks complemented by another 1,500 from a Czech line between 1973 and 1978, and an unknown number from a North Korean line that is currently producing tanks for the domestic and continued export markets.

The T-62 is still in very widespread service, and continues as one of the Warsaw Pact forces' most important first-line assets. The standard features of the tank include an NBC system, active night-vision equipment and a snorkel to permit wading to a maximum depth of 5.5m (18.05ft), and its adequate range on internal fuel can be boosted by auxiliary fuel carried in main and supplementary external tankage. The T-62 has been used extensively in combat, especially in the Middle East. The type has acquitted itself well, the high level of protection provided by its well-sloped armour. However, in common with other Soviet tanks, this protective capability is made all the more valuable by the main armament's poor elevation arc. The T-62 is also limited in offensive capability by its comparatively simple fire-control system.

Given its importance and longevity, it is hardly surprising that the T-62 has appeared in variant form, although few in number. The most important of these in numerical terms is the T-62A, which has a turret of revised shape and different size, together with a rotating cupola mounting (plus external 12.7mm/0.5in machine-gun) in place of the fixed loader's hatch of the T-62. It is also believed that an improved fire-control system and night-vision equipment have been fitted, the former to a standard comparable with that of the M60A3 with a ballistic computer, laser rangefinder and various sensors. A derivative of the T-62A is the T-62M with 'live' tracks for longer life and better performance.

Like the Americans and other major tank-producing nations, the USSR operated on the principle of starting the search for a successor as soon as any major type had entered production. In the case of the T-62 this process led to the development of the T-64. Several prototypes were trialled in the period up to 1966, when the decision was made to place the best in production as the T-64, which was designated the M1970 in Western terminology. It is uncertain when the T-64 began to enter service, but the type is believed to have been manufactured between 1966 and 1971, although the production line remained open until 1981 for the re-manufacture of earlier vehicles. Total production is thought to have been in the order of 8,000 vehicles. Taken in combination, factors such as a comparatively small production run, a late service entry date and an extensive re-manufacturing programme suggest that there were severe problems with the type. It is also probable that the Soviets had a high expectation of the type, which resulted in re-manufacture rather than cancellation of the project.

The initial M1970 version was probably a large-scale pre-production type with a turret basically similar to that of the T-64, but with a different hull, running gear and engine. The turret was located slightly farther to the rear, and the welded hull used a more advanced type of armour than the rolled plate used in the T-62. Whereas the T-54 and its immediate successors used medium-diameter road wheels without track-return rollers, the M1970 and its progeny have six small-diameter road wheels per side instead of the earlier tanks' five larger wheels, four track-return rollers per side to support the inside of the track, and hydropneumatic rather than torsion bar

The Merkava is one of the most advanced tanks in the world, and reflects the virtually unique experience of the Israeli army in fighting four major armoured campaigns since the creation of Israel in 1948.

suspension. The idlers were at the front, leaving the drive sprockets to be located at the rear, where they were powered by hydraulically-assisted transmission driven by a new type of engine, a five-cylinder opposed-piston diesel engine. The M1970 was armed with a 115mm (4.53in) smooth-bore gun, but the T-64 'definitive' production version has a 125mm (4.92in) D-81TM Rapira 3 (or 2A46) smooth-bore gun, an altogether more powerful weapon fitted with an automatic loader to allow a reduction in crew from the M1970's four to the T-64's three. The gun is stabilized in two axes, has a larger-than-usual elevation arc and is used with an advanced fire-control system including a ballistic computer, stabilized optics and a laser rangefinder. Other standard features are an NBC system, night-vision equipment and a snorkel for deep wading; it is also possible that a laser-warning receiver is fitted to provide the crew with advanced warning of attack by a tank fitted with a laser rangefinder, or by an air-launched 'smart' weapon with passive laser guidance to home onto any tank laser-illuminated by a third party.

There were considerable problems associated with the T-64's engine, suspension, automatic loader and fire-control system, and the type has evolved through a number of variants known only by their hybrid Western designations. Thus the initial T-64 was followed by the T-64A (M1981/1) with a revised gunner's sight, smoke-grenade dispensers on the turret and hinges for the attachment of skirt armour; there is also an M1981/2 subvariant fitted with permanent skirts rather than for the optional skirts of the M1981/1.

The next variant is believed to have been the most important production model, built as such but perhaps supplemented by older tanks re-manufactured to the improved standard. This variant is the T-64B, which has the improved 125mm (4.92in) weapon also carried by the T-72 and T-80, together with a revised and more reliable automatic loading system. The gun can also fire the AT-8 'Songster' missile, which is a dual-role weapon for use against tanks to a range of 4,000m (4,375yds) and against helicopters to a range of perhaps 8,000m (8,750yds). The missile is carried in the automatic loader in two sections, and fed into the main ordnance in exactly the same way as conventional ammunition. The precise balance of missiles

Reconnaissance for heavy armoured forces calls for a comparatively light and moderately protected vehicle whose survival is provided by levels of speed and agility greater than those of the more heavily gunned vehicles it may encounter, and by a main gun of larger calibre and greater strength than those carried by faster opponents. The British specialist in this important field is Alvis, which produces a number of tracked and wheeled vehicles characterized by the use of highly reliable commercial, rather than specifically military, components in their automotive systems.

139

and conventional ammunition will depend on the tactical situation, but it is likely that at least some tanks in any given unit will be tasked with a primary anti-helicopter role and therefore will field a higher-than-normal complement of missiles.

The T-64B became operational in 1980, with reactive armour first appearing in 1984. The problems faced by the T-64 series persuaded the Soviet authorities to attempt a comparable but lower-risk version, powered by a conventional diesel engine and fitted with torsion bar suspension for an arrangement of six larger-diameter road wheels on each side, together with only three track-return rollers. The hull was revised accordingly, with slightly less length, marginally more width and a modestly increased height. The result is the T-72, a main battle tank similar to the T-64 in operational capability, but offering greater reliability in its automotive system and, as a result of its lighter weight and improved power-to-weight ratio, superior mobility and performance.

The T-72 began to reach service operators in 1981, and is still in production at four former-Soviet plants and at plants in Czechoslovakia, India, Poland and the former Yugoslavia. Whereas the T-64 is used exclusively by the Russians, the T-72 has no provision for AT-8 missiles and is operated by the Warsaw Pact countries and non-Warsaw Pact operators such as Algeria, former Yugoslavia, Angola, Cuba, Finland, India, Iraq, Libya and Syria.

The T-72 has been developed in a number of forms and variants, and while some of these are known by their Soviet designations, others are best individualized by Western designations. The baseline model is the T-72 discussed above, and has an infra-red searchlight to the left of the main gun; there is also a T-72K command model. The T-72M is the main production variant, with the searchlight moved to the right of the main gun; there is also a T-72MK command model. The designation T-72 (M1981/2) is used for older T-72s retrofitted with side armour to prevent effective top attack of the engine compartment. The T-74 has been produced in several subvariants. The initial version lacks the optics port in the right-hand side of the turret front (presumably for a laser rangefinder), while the T-74 (M1980/1) is similar but has fabric skirt armour over the suspension and side containers. The T-74 (M1981/3) has appeared in two models, the initial type resembling the T-72 (M1980/1) but with thicker frontal armour, and the later type having smoke-grenade launchers. The latest model is the T-74 (T-72 M1984 or T-74M) based on the previous type but with appliqué armour and anti-radiation cladding.

The last main battle tank from the Soviet stable was the T-80, which is now known to be a further development of the missile-capable T-64B, and began to enter production in the early 1980s for service deliveries in 1984. By the end of 1987, it is believed that some 7,000 T-80s had been produced exclusively for the Soviet forces.

The tank is similar in configuration and shape to the T-64, with the driver's compartment at the front, the two-man turret in the centre and the engine compartment at the rear. But the T-80 has a considerable number of detail differences from the T-64B. The most important of these are a laminated glacis for improved protection against kinetic and chemical attack, a dozer blade retracting under the nose, a new pattern of road wheel with torsion bar suspension, a cast steel turret with an inside layer of 'special armour', a modified commander's hatch, revised stowage on the outside of the turret, a modified rear decking and, perhaps most significantly of all, a new powerplant in the form of a 985shp (734ekW) gas turbine with a manual transmission featuring five forward gears and one reverse, compared with the diesel-engined T-64's synchromesh transmission with seven forward gears and one reverse.

The T-64 and T-80 are currently the most important main battle tank types in former Soviet service, but are more than ably backed by massive numbers of T-72s and T-62s.

The Leopard II is the truly formidable battle tank mainstay of the German army, and offers an excellent blend of firepower, protection and mobility.

Glossary

APPLIQUÉ type of armour that is added for extra protection over the baseline armour, and often spaced slightly from the baseline armour

BARBETTE raised and fixed part of the superstructure carrying the fighting compartment or, in heavy tanks of the 1930s, a turret designed to fire over a smaller turret located forward of it

BUSTLE overhanging rear part of the turret helping to balance the weight of the gun and generally containing radio equipment or, in later tanks, main gun ammunition and/or an automatic loader

CUPOLA raised one- or two-man position providing improved fields of vision

FASCINE bundle of chain-wrapped wooden rods (or other contrivance of the same basic shape) for release into a trench or other such obstacle to fill it and so create a pathway

GLACIS downward-sloping plate of frontal armour

GUN weapon designed primarily to deliver direct (and therefore flat) fire

HOWITZER weapon designed primarily to deliver indirect (and therefore high-trajectory) fire

MANTLET piece of armour protecting the open space where the main gun emerges from the turret

MONOCOQUE type of structure in which the 'single shell' skin bears the primary structural loads, thereby removing the need for a conventional chassis

MUZZLE BRAKE arrangement of baffles of similar traps at the muzzle to catch some of the propellant gases and thus reduce the recoil force

MUZZLE VELOCITY the velocity at which a projectile leaves the muzzle of the gun

RE-ENTRANT spot in which armour panels slope inward to create a dangerous shot trap

SHELL projectile containing explosive and therefore combining chemical with kinetic energies for its effect

SHOT solid projectile containing no explosive and securing its effect by kinetic energy alone

SKIRT ARMOUR thin plate armour for the protection of the upper and central parts of the tracks and the tank's running gear

SPALL splinters knocked off the interior of the armour by the impact of a bullet, shell or shot on the outside

SPLASH fragment of bullet entering the interior of the tank after being semi-liquefied by its impact with the rim of the opening

SPONSON position on the side of a tank for the accommodation of a gun and/or a machine-gun

TRACK SHOE individual plate connected by a hinged attachment to its neighbours to create the tank track

TURRET revolving unit carrying the tank's main armament, fighting crew and often part of the secondary armament in the form of a co-axial machine-gun and/or an overhead machine-gun

Index

358.1
Cha
Chant, C.
Armoured fighting vehicles of
the 20th century